AMAZING
GRAINS

Other Books by Joanne Saltzman
Romancing the Bean:
Essentials for Creating Vegetarian Bean Dishes

AMAZING GRAINS

CREATING VEGETARIAN MAIN DISHES WITH WHOLE GRAINS

by Joanne Saltzman

Founder, School of Natural Cookery

H J Kramer Inc
Tiburon, California

To Our Readers
The books we publish are our contribution to an emerging world
based on cooperation rather than on competition, on affirmation
of the human spirit rather than on self-doubt, and on the certainty
that all humanity is connected. Our goal is to touch as many
lives as possible with a message of hope for a better world.
Hal and Linda Kramer, Publishers

Text Copyright © 1990 by Joanne Saltzman
Illustrations Copyright © 1990 by Tina Cash

H J Kramer Inc
P.O. Box 1082
Tiburon, CA 94920

Library of Congress Cataloging in Publication Data

Saltzman, Joanne, 1948–
    Amazing grains : creating vegetarian main dishes with whole grains
/ Joanne Saltzman.
        p.   cm.
    ISBN 0-915811-21-9 : $12.95
    1. Cookery (Cereals)   2. Vegetarian cookery.   3. Entrées (Cookery)
I. Title.
TX808.S25   1990
641.6'31—dc20   89-63725
                                                          CIP

Editor: Jay Harlow
Cover Design and Art: Tina Cash
Book Illustrations: Tina Cash
Editorial Assistant: Nancy Grimley Carleton
Book Production: Schuettge and Carleton
Typesetting: Classic Typography
Manufactured in the United States of America
10 9 8 7 6 5 4

DEDICATION
To all people
as they nourish their creative power
and rejuvenate their beings with whole grain.

THANKS

As I look back to the moments without which this
book wouldn't be here, I am drawn into heartfelt thanks to:

My parents, who let me perform dinners for them at a very early age; and my
dance mentor, the late Nancy Hauser, for developing my independence with creativity.

The late George Oshawa, for inspiration to take charge of my own healing
process with fitness and food; and Tim Rea, the first sponsor of the cooking school,
for allowing me to practice theories of cookery with students of all levels.

Kiril Sokoloff, whose brief encounter with me left reverberating words of courage:
"Go to it!"; Susan Van Auken, the late William Sanford, Dr. Hunter Lilly,
Alice Price, and John Molfese, for helping me capture this process onto paper; and
Marta Bean, Margaret Walker, Johrei, and Trise Cruea, for their ever-present support.

Shelly Zucker, Harriet Chorney, June McElroy, Laurie Ogletree,
David Kraft, and John Gritton, for scrutinizing the recipes; and all the
students of the School of Natural Cookery, for sharing their creativity.

Steve Gorad, Anne Redfield, Sylvia Keepers, Texas A&M University,
Eden Foods, Maskal Teff, and Lundberg Family Farms, who shared their
resources of information on grain.

And most gratefully to my publishers, Hal and Linda Kramer, for their kindness
and their courage to see the potential for a book in a sketchy collection of ideas;
and Jay Harlow and Elaine Ratner, who understood *Amazing Grains* and took on
the project of editing this book while involved in writing their own cookbook.

CONTENTS

MILLET (contd.)

OATS

QUINOA

RICE

AMARANTH

JOB'S TEARS

TEFF

SAUCES

CHARTS AND WORKSHEETS

Introduction

The kitchen radiated a peaceful warmth; my teacher was quietly attentive as she gently moved little gems around the skillet with a bamboo rice paddle. She appeared to be in a trance, her hand tracing a spiral pattern over and over again, not changing direction until, as if a messenger entered her being, the bamboo paddle shifted to a vertical motion, flattening each grain against the heavy cast-iron pan. Then the spiral began again, this pattern repeated until the grains were dry and resembled giant grains of sand, each holding the full potential to rejuvenate my life. Caught in the aroma of roasting rice, I fell in love with grain.

I was hooked. How could such a simple food as brown rice emit such a divine character? Each grain was a twin to its neighbor yet individual and whole by itself. The peace and warmth that surrounded this treatment drew me into a magical realm of cooking.

I want to tell you a story. This is a true story and indirectly the reason this book was written.

It was during a turbulent year in college in the 1960s that I first became aware of my ignorance. I ate a common collegiate diet: donuts, coffee, and jelly beans. I shared a house with three young women who all loved to cook. We celebrated each Friday night with baking contests. A large group of friends brought brownies, pies, cakes, etc. I was a dance major at the time. As I look back it seems like cooking, eating, and dancing were what my life was about. They also became the theme of my education.

The university dance studio was located at the top of an ancient edifice. The only way to get there was up a noisy old elevator and down a long narrow hallway. Alone with a friend, waiting for the afternoon class to begin, I sat quietly outside the studio, bemoaning our need to create "real" art. We wanted to express dance that was potent enough to make a difference at a time in history when protesters were making a stand against the Vietnam War and Martin Luther King's speeches were igniting a sense of freedom.

Out of nowhere, a young bat flew at us. Barefoot, leaping, jumping, and screaming, we drew attention from the classroom. The studio door opened just as the bat bit my little toe. The thought of it gagged me. I stopped screaming and was presented with the little bat by a large bald man with a hammer in hand. He handed me the bat and suggested I go immediately to the Health Service. "See if the bat is rabid," he said. The Health Service was closed at 4:30 that particular Friday, so the bat stayed in my locker for the weekend.

The doctors convinced me I needed to receive rabies serum or I could die. Two weeks later I was chained to a hospital bed with intravenous tubes. My well-trained dancer's body swelled and my skin was covered with huge red welts. Doctors injected me with horse serum, duck embryo, and sugar water and fed me jello, spam, and instant mashed potatoes. If you have ever been really depressed, you will have a hint of how I felt. Depression is not my nature. I began to ask questions. My inquiry revealed that the doctors didn't know anything; they were waiting for something to happen; the bat wasn't rabid. Apparently the University Medical School had developed a new rabies serum, and I was to be the guinea pig.

Depression turned to anger and frustration. Inspired by a little book my sister gave me, I was determined to heal my troubled body and spirit myself. The book, George Oshawa's *Zen Macrobiotics,* called for the things I did best — dancing, cooking, and eating. Ready to take responsibility for my life, I left the hospital without being discharged. Dramatic and fearless, this action was the premier of my personal power. It felt great!

I was thrilled to dispel medical toxins by dancing and to nourish my body with whole, fresh foods — whole grains, fresh vegetables, beans, nuts, seeds, and complex sugars. My body soon returned to normal. I was cooking with an awareness of "the whole." Choosing a carrot or onion became a thought process. I learned that by using whole grains I could absorb energy that wouldn't be available if the grain was cut, crushed, or milled into flour. The energy of a whole food radiates differently from that of foods that are not whole. Once the food has been altered it loses some of its natural power. Whole-grain pasta, breads, and cereals are valuable foods, but whole grains in their simplicity and wholeness are healing.

This book is not suggesting another diet, or even that you eat only whole grains. You are most likely already aware that whole grains and fresh natural foods are healing and powerful. *Amazing Grains* is intended to clear the fog of confusion about how to prepare them, but, more importantly, I hope it will eliminate boredom and support your personal expression in food.

Do you ever wish you could simply walk into the kitchen and put together a masterpiece with whatever is there? Have you ever been caught short of ingredients for a special recipe and felt a trip through the rain, sleet, or snow to the store was the only solution? When you learn this system of creative cooking, you will no longer hesitate to try a new variation on a successful dish or resist the temptation toward a new creation for lack of understanding the variables of cooking grain. Your personal expression and power will flourish.

HOW TO USE THIS BOOK

Amazing Grains is really two books in one. It is a book of recipes, and it is a discussion of the process through which these recipes came about.

The recipes are everyday, easy, sometimes elegant dishes. I hope you will use them in two ways. One, enjoy their simple preparation, and, two, consider them examples to help you understand how the different styles of dishes are put together.

The "process" that follows each recipe gives you the fundamentals for creativity by breaking it into its elements: cooking method, cooking liquid, salt seasoning, oil, etc. Once you understand the function of these elements and the techniques of the cooking methods, you will be able to create your own dishes with whatever ingredients you have at hand.

Charts offer quick references when you are inventing a grain dish.

Worksheets (see Appendix) reinforce the thoughts behind the creative process of cooking with whole grains and sauces. They guide you through the process and allow you to record what you make.

Part I
Cooking Creatively
With Whole Grains

Why Whole Grains?

The Power of Grains

Are grains a perfect food? Almost. It has been said that man can survive on bread and water alone. Whole grains contain the majority of basic nutrients essential for life in humans and animals: water, carbohydrates, fats, protein, vitamins, minerals, and fiber. This miracle food not only has full capacity to reproduce itself a thousandfold, but it can be stored and transported without damage or spoilage. Grains found in ancient tombs have retained enough life force to sprout and reproduce after thousands of years. There is no mistake that grain reigns as king of all food groups for animals as well as people. Grains even offer themselves as home to living organisms in fermented foods that have been staples, such as bread and beer since 3000 B.C. and more recently including wine, vinegar, and the soybean salt seasonings (miso and shoyu).

In Greek mythology, grain is associated with Demeter, the archetypal mother of the human soul and the fruitful forces of nature. Her initiations of earth rituals founded harvesting cultures in the transition from nomadic to homesteading life-styles. The new agriculture wasn't just growing grains for cattle; people ate them, which brought about a new social structure. Indirectly, grains were responsible for the first alphabet and arithmetic systems. To Demeter, grain was a tool for opening new consciousness, containing the force of mother's milk; rooting itself in the earth, it carried the forces of life through stem and ear to open to the cosmic forces of the sun. It was believed that by the Demeterian creative force, seven grains arose from the virgin fertile earth: wheat, rye, oats, barley, millet, rice, and corn, some time around 12,000 B.C. Each in its own way strives to connect with the higher worlds through mineralization.

"Culture of the fields made possible culture of the minds."

Harold McGee
On Food and Cooking

Bread Grains vs. Dish Grains

Botanically, "grain" covers around 8,000 species of grasses, although humans eat only a few of them. Please note that the term "grain" as used in this book does not refer exclusively to the botanical family *Gramineae* (Grass family). Quinoa, amaranth, wild rice, and buckwheat, included here, are sometimes called "pseudocereals"; they act like grain but are from different botanical families. They are included because of how they are prepared and how they function in a meal. The term "whole-grain dishes" refers to dishes made with all the parts of the seeds' anatomical structure: the pericarp, endosperm, and germ. (See diagram, p. 192.)

I like to distinguish "bread grains" (wheat, rye, barley, and corn) from "dish grains" (buckwheat, millet, oats, quinoa, and rice). Because bread grains are inherently tough, they require some kind of processing for them to be usable in the digestive tract. From the beginning, the most common treatment has been milling and cracking, first with hand-held stones to crush the tough layers of grain and later with a water-powered mill. The resulting flour or meal could then be made into bread, pasta, crackers, chips, or ground cereals. Whole wheat, whole rye, whole barley, and whole dried corn respond to the treatments of dish grains, but I find it almost unbearable to sit down to a bowl of these grains cooked whole. However, they can be most appealing served whole when mixed in small amounts with dish grains.

As civilization continued to refine daily life, so was daily bread refined, by throwing away nutritive parts of the grain and keeping the starch. The lighter, the whiter, and the longer the shelf life, the better. Wheat germ was too dangerous, drawing potential rancidity, and bran made bread too heavy. This is an old story today, in a time when awareness of food's power has had a great effect on the American people's choice of bread. Reports that in the past decade American people have purchased one-third less white bread than in previous decades indicate the direction of a whole-grain market (Harold McGee, *On Food and Cooking*).

It's hard for me to believe that ancient cultures milled and cracked all their grain when dish grains (buckwheat, millet, oats, quinoa, and rice) are so incredibly delicious left whole. In this book, I want to address the wholeness of grains. There is something in their wholeness that speaks clearly. Remember Buckminster Fuller's expression of the sixties "The whole is greater than the sum of its parts." As new awareness in food brings new consciousness, I feel it is time to explore the full potential of whole-grain dishes. Could there be more power in a dish made with whole grains if the whole is greater than the sum of its parts? We can begin to understand this from two directions, scientific nutrition and energetics.

Energetics and the Spirit of Grain

"A force resides in a grain of cereal. This is the force which enables a seed to develop into a plant. Nature can awaken this force; man today cannot."

Rudolf Steiner, cited in *The Dynamics of Nutrition* Gerhard Schmidt

Whole grains and other plants hold an inner strength, a special harmony of earth, water, air, and fire (sun energy). Nature's elements produce "natural food"; the closer the food is to these elements when we eat it, the more nature's powerful energetic qualities will be passed on.

Energetics is a way to think about the quality of food. It determines the amount of life force food contains and the amount of energy that it can give. Energetics is concerned with where food has been and how it has grown. Looking at the energetics of a food gives us a perspective of wholeness in relation to the universe and helps determine sound nutrition. Most importantly, it is easily understood through intuition.

Today, as in the time of the earliest Greek civilizations, grain has a reputation of being spiritual food. As the foundation of vegetarian diets, grains are a link between the mineral and animal kingdoms from which humans draw nourishment. Earth provides vital elements for human development in the form of minerals, but our human systems are not conditioned to digest inert minerals. Plants digest minerals. They thrive on the quality of soil, which is determined by the mineral content. Plants grow by balancing the energy forces of earth and heaven, transforming inert minerals into food for animals and people. When humans eat plants, they receive the synthesis of earth energy from the mineral kingdom and spiritual energy from the cosmos. Animals also eat plants; horses, cows, camels, whales, gorillas, and elephants are all pure vegetarians, with strong bodies and peaceful characters. It's not surprising that spiritual practices require a vegetarian diet, or the reverse, that a vegetarian diet will awaken one's spirit and intuition.

If we can clean up our taste buds and olfactory sensors, we won't have to "think" about what we eat. Our tastes and choices in cooking will guide us to rely on our instincts and common sense when making nutritional choices.

> "The Goddess brought us the fruits of the fields by virtue of which we were able to make the transition from animal life to human life; then she brought us the initiations which enable those allowed to participate to face with hope the end of life and all existence."
>
> Isocrates, cited in
> *The Dynamics of Nutrition*
> Gerhard Schmidt

> "Taste and smell are chemical senses by which we sample the chemical composition of our surroundings and our food. Because nutrition is a matter of finding and ingesting particular chemical compounds, some such sense has been a necessity from the very beginnings of life. Even single-cell organisms must have a way of discriminating between useful and harmful molecules."
>
> Harold McGee
> *On Food and Cooking*

Quality

The importance of grain in human survival is evident when we consider the capacity for this food to sustain its life force. For example, consider an experiment that was conducted by the International Nature Farm Research Center in Atami City, Japan, to compare the life force of samples of chemically grown rice and organically grown rice. For seven years these grains were sealed. In the beginning they were equal in volume. After seven years, the organic grain still filled the jar and maintained its color and shape; the chemically grown grain filled only half the jar and was like tar in color and shape. It became clear through this demonstration that organic soil produces food with a quality of energy more vital than chemical soil. Foods grown in natural conditions have more power than foods that have been chemically treated, but what does this show about the energetic power of grain? Do you know any other group of food that has the capacity to hold its character force seven years? This shows why grains are so special, why they have been the foundation of civilizations, and why they are worthy of eating whole.

When you discover grain has many B vitamins, vitamin E, lots of complex carbohydrates, fiber, and protein, and you have an idea that this is good, you may choose to eat grain. You might choose to eat whole grain or processed grain. To modern science grain is grain and it will carry this nutritive value whether it is precooked, polished, bleached, milled, or mixed with other good or not-so-good ingredients. Even if this processing doesn't change the nutritional value (manufacturers insure nutritional elements by adding vitamin and mineral enrichments to replace what has been lost in processing), it drastically changes the energetic quality of a whole grain. A whole food is not equal to the sum of its parts. We can't take food apart and expect it to be as energetically valuable as a living food, whose properties come from the balance of heaven and earth forces.

I find it easier to select foods by their energetic quality than by the nutritional symbols of vitamins, minerals, fiber, and protein. For instance, oat bran is getting plenty of press these days, so manufacturers are busy scraping the bran off the whole oat groat, and people are trying to figure out how much of this nonfood to eat. If I want oat bran, I eat the *whole* oat groat; intuition tells me how much to eat, and I receive much, much more than processed bran. Or, in order to have a balanced diet, I choose to eat a variety of fresh whole foods, each of which represents a different kind of growing style (energy) and color. Variety is the key to a balanced diet.

Color gives our visual senses a way to determine the power in food. We ask, "Is it ripe? Are they vibrant or dull?" Using our visual sense we see if food is dehydrated, shriveled, spoiled, or molding. Color is usually the first qualification. Harlan Lundberg from Lundberg Family Farms (rice growers in the Sacramento Valley) reads the energy of the plants in the field; he is particularly interested in rice that has a deep color. "Unscientifically, these characteristics go beyond a commodity." Harlan watches the grains grow; he feels there is more nutrition, more food power, in grains with a rich color.

Whole Grains in the Body

Concepts of nutrition and natural science separate a food into individual elements for analysis. Each food is categorized for a specific function in relation to the body's requirements of these elements. Even though this system of thought is in its infant stages and very complicated, it is a common concern shaping opinions of what to eat. In general, people are very confused about what to eat; at least there is some agreement that what goes in the body has some effect on how the body functions. Grains are associated with starch, which in turn brings concern for high calories and stored fat. It is true that a refined grain product like white flour stays in the body turning starch to fat, but whole grains work much differently. Whole grains are valued for carbohydrate, protein, vitamins, minerals, natural fat, and fiber; when all these elements are eaten together, they work in balance, and are eliminated by cooperative effort. A refined grain product doesn't have all the nutrients available to assist the starch in its process of nurturing the body. Instead it must draw nutrients from other sources within the body, or additives (enriched, fortified, additional fiber) become essential and weaken the energetic quality. Let's take a quick look at how the elements of cooked whole dish grains work in the body.

CARBOHYDRATES. These are the elements that help us get out of bed, move around, walk, run, etc. They translate into pure energy for the body. Through photosynthesis, a process that transforms sun energy into chemical energy, plants nourish us with carbon, hydrogen, and oxygen. These elements play important roles in the body's nerve tissues, and in the hormone and immune systems. Carbohydrates are primarily starch, sugar, and cellulose, and are found in grain, beans, vegetables, and fruit.

PROTEIN. When we cut a finger, tear a muscle, lose a nail, or our hair falls out, protein is the component that rebuilds the tissues; it is the healer of bulk in the body. Chains of amino acids link together in varying proportions. Some grains (quinoa, amaranth) excel in their amino acid count, while others (rice, buckwheat) shine in vitamin and mineral content. This is another great reason to alternate grain dishes.

WATER. The average human's body weight is 60 percent water. Most of this fluid lies within the cells; the remaining liquid transports nutrients and waste and acts as a lubricant. Cooked brown rice contains 70 percent water.

MINERALS. These powerful earth elements move the body fluids. They affect nerve impulses and enzymatic reactions. I think of them as the great policemen, watching over our state of being. From grain we receive varied proportions of sodium, potassium, calcium, magnesium, phosphorus, iron, copper, manganese, zinc, and molybdenum. By adding a pinch of sea salt to the first-stage cooking methods, we take in vital trace minerals from the sea.

VITAMINS. These are the great helpers. They help in the process of life within the body, assisting growth, repair, and general cellular activity. The rich supply of B vitamins found in whole grain is chief executive over processing carbohydrates, protein, and fat throughout the body.

FIBER. This is not a nutrient, but provides the valuable service of softening and giving bulk to the waste products of digestion, thereby easing their elimination from the body. Accumulation of fiber triggers a response in the lower canal to signal elimination.

FATS. These slow the digestive process and act as a reserve energy source. Nature gives grain a small amount, usually placed in the germ. Whole oats have the highest fat content, are slow burning in the body, and provide extra energy.

Variety: The Key to Good Health

A shocking pattern has come about in the last century. This pattern shows a lack of diversity in the foods we eat, more specifically monotony in the seeds that produce food. The trend to hybridize seeds to acquire a uniform look, standard color, and long-term shelf life has sacrificed the seeds' ability to survive insect attacks and extreme weather conditions. Seeds have become inbred, unable to reproduce their own seed. Gardeners and farmers have become dependent on (chemical) seed companies, but more importantly hybridizing eliminates the tremendous variety available through genetically undisturbed foods (Dr. Allen Kaplur, *Peace Seeds*). Malnutrition exists in a perfect diet (whatever that may be for you) if the seeds from which the foods are grown are genetically repeated. For example, wheat and corn and their by-products are consumed in overriding popularity to an extreme where 1 out of 10 people has a sensitivity or allergy to these foods at one time or another.

Looking at grains, we see myriad "kinds" of rice; quinoa also has thousands of strains, and millet has 6,000 variations around the world—

reddish brown millet in Nepal, old strains (pearl millet) in North Africa, and the yellow-gold variety in the United States. New grains (from old traditions) will be arriving in the forthcoming years. Recently, the smallest grain in the world, teff, came to market. As other grains, including sorghum and pearl millet, come into the market, our options for whole-grain cookery will expand further.

If nature had one perfect food, would we eat just that food? I doubt it. There is something in the principle of variety that nourishes our inner souls. It's called creativity. When you employ the information from *Amazing Grains,* you will be able to prepare any grain in its whole state, but more importantly you will have the tools for creatively using a variety of foods and a variety of cooking methods to keep you in good health.

The Creative Process

My experience is that by cooking creatively with grains you can gain access to the intuitive part of you, which in return guides you to appropriate choices on what to eat. Whole grains are so very simple and bland, they provide a blank canvas on which to create culinary wonders with color, taste, aroma, and texture. Eating and cooking come naturally to all of us and creativity is a given at birth. Put the two together, and I know that *anyone* can be a food artist. Cooking feeds more than the hunger of an empty stomach; it can nourish the soul. The old saying "The way to a man's [human's] heart is through his [or her] stomach" suggests that a carefully prepared meal is an expression of love. Cooking draws on our natural instincts and confirms that we are sensual beings. Through left-brain understanding of the possibilities and right-brain courage to follow our imaginations, we can all become food artists, able to give an energy transfusion through the purity of whole grains to ourselves and other people we love.

Finding the Courage for Creativity

I have heard the expressions "right brain" and "left brain" for years, but recently another significant piece of the brain, the corpus callosum, was brought to my attention. It's the piece that connects the two halves of the brain, a tunnel or bridge by which messages pass from one side to the other and back again. Thrilled with this discovery, I immediately tried to consciously gain access to my right brain, then my left. What I found was that I really needed to trust that the right brain would show up. I had to be willing to stop my left brain from thinking, so that messages from the right would surface. I never knew exactly what the right side was saying, but the messages must have crossed the bridge, because ideas came bounding forth.

In a lecture by Joseph Chilton Pearce, I heard that the right brain makes choices that are appropriate for our well-being; it knows how to safely use the information in the left brain, which has knowledge of the possibilities. Understanding general nutrition, cooking methods, and the character and quality of ingredients feeds the left brain valuable information to support the appropriate choices from the right brain, the home of intuition.

Until now, I have always had a vague thought that the ancients who brought grain to fruition knew best how to prepare it. But through the creative process I have reached a level of satisfaction beyond any preconceived idea of preparing whole dish grains.

"Each and every person is creative. Awakening personal creativity begins with the courage and curiosity to be open to oneself beyond the preconceived ideas of who we are – who we should be. It takes a willingness to listen to oneself and honestly recognize one's true needs, wants and desires. It takes commitment and energy to bring fulfillment to the self, then personal creativity is available. When one understands this, it is clear that being creative is the ultimate nourishment."

Roberta Frediani,
Founder of Transformational
Healing Institute

FOODS TO HAVE ON HAND

GRAINS
Buckwheat Groats
Oats
  Steel Cut
  Whole
  Rolled
Millet
Quinoa
Brown Rice
  Short Grain
  Medium Grain
  Long Grain
  Basmati
  Sweet
  Wehani
  Wild
Teff
Amaranth
Job's Tears

SALT SEASONINGS
Sea Salt
Vegetable Sea Salt
Miso
  Rice
  Barley
  Buckwheat
  Red, White, Yellow
  Chickpea
Tamari
Shoyu
Umeboshi
  Whole Plum
  Paste
  Vinegar
Sauerkraut
Olives

COOKING LIQUID
Water
Juice
  Apple
  Orange
  Cranberry
  Lemon

I want to share with you the magical process that happens when I invent new dishes or have to cook from the cupboard. Even though an explanation of left-brain information fills this entire book, the actual event of creation is simple; it happens in a split second. It takes practice to reach a level of skill in any art form, but it could happen at any moment no matter what your experience. Trust yourself, and practice the cooking methods in this book with all the grains; try a variety of seasonings and sauces to become familiar with their characters. The recipes only serve as guides for you to experience these foods and cooking methods. It's the process following the recipe that will guide you to personal expression and freedom. Study both; your moment will come. It could take six days or six months, but once you "have it," this cooking skill will be with you a lifetime. In this fast-paced world, knowledge, experience, and intuition will enable you to prepare healthy food fast, so you won't need to rely on "fast foods"—even the ones marketed as "healthy."

Tapping "The Process" in You

In "the process," you need only know two pieces of information. One, what food you are cooking, and, two, the cooking method you will employ. How much of each ingredient you need to use is not as important in "the process" as in recipes, because knowing the cooking methods and knowing the character and function of ingredients allows your instincts to tell you how much you will need. If this alarms you, take comfort in knowing that you have all the information you need to take care of yourself. Much of it is stored in the right brain, a place that determines with intelligence how much of what is appropriate.

The process laid out in this book is like a game, a mix-and-match game. Ingredients are categorized by grain, cooking liquids, salt seasonings, oils, nuts and seeds, main vegetables, decorative vegetables, and herbs and spices. Each group has a special function, and each food within that group has a special character. When I have only one ingredient on hand from a category, and I need that ingredient because it functions a certain way in a particular cooking method, then I have little choice but to use it. Usually I try to have more than one ingredient on hand from each category. The more ingredients on hand from each category, the more variety and balance in your diet.

After choosing a cooking method and ingredients, select a sauce style. If you don't want to use a sauce, select decorative or major vegetables, herbs, and spices. That's it. It's fun and very freeing.

Once you have mastered this simple process, you can look at any other recipe, break it into ingredients and cooking methods, and record it in your memory as a great resource for your information bank. I do this in restaurants, at parties, or anywhere I enjoy a dish and want to re-create it. If you eat a dish that you really like, the memory of its taste, texture, and presentation are stored in the right brain. As you become more aware of the powers of the right brain, you will notice tastes, textures, and presentations of dishes that you have eaten and have memories about. Some of these may be more pleasant than others. Practice with this process will enable you to record and reproduce any dish you have eaten, whether it is fancy restaurant food or down-home cooking.

If you get stuck, if your left brain is too full of technical information on cooking methods and ingredients to make a decision, try this technique for leaping into creativity:

- Look at the food you are considering working with. Be willing for your left brain to stop asking what is possible. Move across the bridge or through the tunnel into your right brain. Stare at the food until it no longer is in focus and it becomes a blur.
- Stay with the blur. Soon you will notice feelings about the texture and taste of the food you are looking at or the texture and taste you desire. Information may jump from the left brain back to the right and vice versa.
- Soon you should have an idea for beginning your dish. When you have a sense of the texture you desire, the tastes, and the flavors, refer to the charts in this book for quick information, and employ the taste-and-sniff test; the grain cookery chapter will clarify the cooking methods.

Planned Creativity

After studying the variety of cooking methods and the characteristics that result from them, you can shift the process to the creative avenue of the right brain. This can be spontaneous or planned creativity. It can be inspired by what lies at hand in the cupboards and refrigerator, or it can jump out at you while you shop in your favorite market. Another source comes from inside—cravings, the body asking for something special.

Stock
Nut Milk
Beer
Wine
  Sherry
  Mirin
Vinegar
  Apple Cider
  Rice
  Wine (Red, White, Flavored)
  Umeboshi
  Raspberry

OIL
Whole Avocado
Corn
Olive, Olives
Peanut
Safflower
Sesame
  Dark
  Light
Sunflower
Walnut
Ghee

NUTS AND SEEDS
Almonds
Cashews
Filberts
Peanuts
Pistachios
Pumpkin Seeds
Sesame Seeds
Sunflower Seeds
Pistachios

BEANS
Pinto
Garbanzo
Black Turtle
Kidney
Lentils
Azuki

VEGETABLES
Kombu Sea Vegetable
Carrots
Onions
Cabbage

Scallions
Celery
Broccoli
Potatoes
Cauliflower
Kale
Collards
Squash
Canned Tomatoes

HERBS
Arugula
Basil
Tarragon
Bay Leaf
Chives
Cilantro
Dill
Fennel
Marjoram
Mint
Oregano
Parsley
Rosemary
Sage
Thyme

SPICES
Nutmeg
Horseradish
Paprika
Pepper (Black, White)
Allspice
Caraway
Cardamom
Cayenne Pepper
Chili Powder
Chinese Five Spice
Cinnamon
Cloves
Coriander
Cumin
Ginger (fresh)
Garlic (fresh)

DECORATIVE
VEGETABLES
Red – Purple
  Sweet Red Peppers
  Red Radish
  Tomato

When cooking from the kitchen, not only can you experience absolute creativity, you can economize food costs. This cooking skill is essential for people with low food budgets or frugal habits. The key to creating successful dishes on the spot with what you have is stocking the pantry properly. Look at the chart entitled "Foods to Have on Hand" (pp. 12–16). Notice that each food category offers a variety of selections. If you have only one item from each category, you will have much repetition in seasoning and a very narrow diet. If you choose two or three items from each category, the possibilities expand to a livable diet. More than four selections from each category award you infinite creations and a well-rounded diet.

Shopping in your favorite market is a great way to stimulate your creativity. If you are letting the market inspire you, enter the store without any idea of what you want. Notice which category of food you are in. What catches your eye? No doubt it is brilliantly fresh or on special. As you shop, keep in mind the different categories of food and which seasoning agents you will be using. This can be an expensive adventure, as a good market will offer a grand variety of seasonings, decorator vegetables, and grains. If your budget is not restricted, you may desire two or more items from each category. If you want to control your desires, stay with only one item from each category, but try things you haven't used before.

If you can tune in, sometimes your body asks for a certain kind of food, and this begins a chain of events in the kitchen. The craving is usually for a specific food or food group. Sometimes it asks for a kind of seasoning or special taste, and other times it is looking for a texture. Gooey, chewy, soft, sweet, pungent, full-bodied. Do you recognize these?

VISUALIZING YOUR DISH

You don't have to visualize a dish in order to create one, but it helps.

Begin by imagining your dish. Learn to trust your inner knowledge about what it is you want. If your mind can't find anything to create, focus on your tongue and salivary glands. What are they looking for?

If you still can't locate an idea, follow this process:

- Look at the charts.
- Pick a grain.
- Choose a preliminary treatment or cooking method that will give you a texture that appeals to you.

- Do you want a sauce?
- What kind of sauce, hot or cold?
- Look at the sauce chart; there are five styles. Which style best suits the texture and presentation of your dish?
- Follow the worksheets to create your dish.
- If you don't want a sauce, select a secondary cooking method.
- Consult your pantry, your taste buds, and the ingredients chapter to determine which seasonings you will use

Things You Need to Know to Work With the Process

COOKING METHODS

Preliminary treatments such as dry-roasting, sautéing, and soaking affect flavor and texture; they make a grain dish distinctive.

First-stage cooking methods include baking, boiling, pressure-cooking, and steeping. Grains cooked by one of these methods need sauces, condiments, vegetables, or herbs and spices. At this stage, altering cooking liquids changes the dish; be daring!

Second-stage cooking methods include braising, marinating, deep-frying, and refrying. Dishes cooked by one of these methods are dependent on decorative vegetables, cooking liquids, oils, and herbs and spices. Hot and cold sauces work well with marinated and deep-fried grains.

USING THE SENSES TO CHOOSE SEASONINGS

If you have no idea which seasonings, herbs, and spices go with what you are making, begin by choosing one of the necessary ingredients. If you are making a cold sauce it could be either an oil or a salt seasoning that you begin with. If it is a hot sauce, begin with the base. Smell or taste the oil, the salt seasoning, or the base of the sauce. Just the very smallest amount will do.

Take an herb or spice you suspect might be a good combination. Crush the herb with your finger tips. Smell the herb while you taste the beginning of your dish. Smelling and tasting will give you a good sense of which seasonings will work together, and which seasonings repel each other.

Red Onion
Purple Cabbage
Beets

Yellow – Orange
Sweet Yellow Pepper
Yellow Summer Squash
Carrots
Corn
Yams
Sweet Potato
Winter Squash
Nasturtium Flowers
Marigold Flowers
Turmeric
Onion Skins

Green
Peas
Green Beans
Green Onions
Zucchini
Green Pepper
Avocado
Celery
Asparagus
Chicory
Kale
Collards
Lettuce

White
White Onions
Fennel
Belgian Endive
Cauliflower
Hearts of Palm
Daikon
Bean Sprouts
Water Chestnut

Black
Burdock Root
Black Sesame Seeds
Black Olives

MISCELLANEOUS
Rice and Barley Malt Syrup
Prepared Mustard
Tomato Paste, Purée
Bouillon

Flour
  Rice
  Oat
  Quinoa
  Whole Wheat
  Whole Wheat Pastry
  Barley
  Corn
Arrowroot

SEASONING WITHOUT MEASURING

Seasoning without measuring is fun; it saves time and sends a glimmer of confidence into your being. It does require a conscious mind and a sort of reasonable approach to the unreasonable. One student shared her grandmother's method of seasoning: "Just keep pouring it on until your conscience hurts."

Look at the size of the pot, bowl, or skillet you are using. Judge whether the grain or sauce is deep or shallow inside it.

Hold the seasoning agent in the hand that you write with and move it steadily back and forth in a zig-zag motion. The slower you move the seasoning and the closer together you move the zig-zag lines, the stronger the flavor will be. If the grain or sauce is shallow, zig-zag only once. If the grain or sauce is deep in the pot, judge the depth as so many times a shallow amount of food and zig-zag the number of shallow depths.

WORKSHEETS AND CHARTS

When you are ready to make your own dishes, you might want to use the worksheets on pages 188–90 to learn and record the process. They are very simple to use. Just make your selections, using the charts as guidelines if necessary, and record your selections in the space provided. Use the following charts, which appear throughout the book, for easy reference:

DEFINITION OF COOKING METHODS FOR GRAIN (pp. 62–63). This chart distinguishes among the cooking methods. It will guide you to choose a cooking method appropriate for the season. For instance, seasonal cooking methods are determined by where the sun is. If it is summer and the sun is out more than in winter, less fire energy is needed. Fire energy is transmitted not only by the duration of fire, but through heat stored in hot oil. Notice that baking and deep-frying are not recommended for summer cooking, when the sun provides us with fire.

TEXTURE CHART (p. 20). This chart explains how to get the texture you desire. It shows which cooking methods work best to achieve your desired texture and what kinds of dishes you can make with that particular texture. The temperatures of the grain and cooking liquid at the onset of the primary cooking method are noted as they have a direct effect on the texture of the finished dish.

FIRST-STAGE COOKING METHODS: LIQUID, GRAIN, AND TIME (p. 74). This chart shows the quantity of liquid needed for each first-stage cooking method, the general volume of yield, and an estimated time for cooking. The yield for each grain is marked, but there is a slight variation in yield between cooking methods. You will discover these with experience. The first number is the amount of cooking liquid; the second number shows the amount of whole grain. All the ratios are in proportion to one part grain. The third number gives an estimated duration of cooking time in minutes. Remember, these are ratios, not measurements in cups. With the exception of the boiling method, don't cook less than one cup of grain.

COOKING LIQUIDS (p. 46). This chart gives you an overview of cooking liquids for whole-grain dishes and sauces. Here you can get a sense of the energy, texture, and flavor of the various liquids and learn which cooking methods they work well with. I have included my favorite ways of using them to guide you to your own experience. Use this chart to verify your knowledge of how these ingredients function.

SALT SEASONINGS (p. 51). This chart is an overview of salt seasonings. It gives a sense of their energy, texture, and flavor. Compatible cooking methods and favorite uses provide guidelines. Use this chart to verify your knowledge of how these ingredients function.

OIL CHART (p. 56). This chart is an overview of the energy, color, and flavor of the great variety of cooking oils. It includes suggestions for compatible cooking methods and favorite uses. Use this chart to verify your knowledge of how the ingredients function.

CHART OF TASTES (pp. 23–24). Sweet, sour, bitter, pungent (hot), and salty are five basic tastes that we all have receptors for in our mouths. This chart is a subjective evaluation of how particular foods register the different tastes.

TRADITIONAL FLAVOR COMBINATIONS (p. 25). This chart shows cultural patterns of combining oil, cooking liquid, herbs, and spices. These were originally based on local availability and trade routes. Now all herbs and spices are available to us, and we can invent combinations that cross established cultural patterns. Don't limit yourself to traditions; be courageous; sniff and taste new possibilities.

CREATING BRAISING LIQUIDS (p. 120). With this chart you can practice mixing and matching ingredients in your mind. Then you can do it with the ingredients in the cupboard.

HOT SAUCES (p. 150). This chart shows the ingredients for five styles of hot sauces. Make one selection from each category to create a sauce.

COLD SAUCES (p. 172). This chart suggests categories of ingredients needed to create cold sauces (including marinades). You may need to use more than one cooking liquid to get the necessary volume.

a Cook

Thoughts From

Creating Texture With Whole Grains

Texture has always been considered an uncontrollable result of the kind of grain that is cooked: long grains come out dry, light, and fluffy while short grains are sticky, heavy, and chewy. This is true if you stick to the most common method of cooking grain (steeping). I invite you to play with the following ideas on creating texture; they should bring you to new dishes and shed a little light on how to avoid or create sticky, heavy, wet, dry, light, or individual grains.

Preliminary treatments (dry-roasting, sautéing, and soaking) and first-stage cooking methods help determine the working texture of a grain dish. The success of second-stage cooking methods depends on the texture that is created in the first-stage method. For instance, grain to be deep-fried should be sticky and clinging together, and marinated grain dishes need open, receptive grains to soak up the seasonings and liquids.

A subtle but most influential factor in controlling texture with grain is temperature—the temperature of the cooking liquid and the temperature of the grain at the onset of first-stage methods. Grain is considered "hot" when it has been dry-roasted or sautéed, and "cold" when it is raw. Combining cold liquid with raw grain can result in a heavy, sticky, and chewy texture. Hot liquid with hot grain creates a light, fluffy, and individual texture. Hot liquid with cold grain or cold liquid with hot grain makes a somewhat chewy yet individual (not sticky) texture. Each grain responds a little differently, but the principles do create a variety of energetics, possibilities of texture, and perhaps most important, they keep the cook engaged in thought and alert, and they offer a way out of routine and boredom.

Cooking Grains With Vegetables and Beans

Vegetables and beans add color, texture, and taste to grain dishes. In the recipes in this book, "major" vegetables refers to those that are cooked with the grain in the first stage; vegetables added after the grain has been cooked are called "decorative" vegetables, because they are mostly used to enhance the color and design appeal of the dish. Special decorative vegetables are listed in the Foods to Have on Hand chart on pages 12–16, but any regular vegetable can be used.

TEXTURE CHART

Preliminary Treatment	Texture	Compatible Cooking Methods	Flavor	Suggestions
DRY-ROAST	Fluffy, light, dry, individual, chewy	Steep, bake, boil, marinate, refry, braise	Full, nutty	Hot liquid
SAUTÉ	Soft, semiheavy, moist, individual	Dry-roast, steep, bake, pressure-cook, refry, braise	Oil bonds vegetable flavors and seasonings to grain	Add vegetables and herbs
SOAK	Extremely soft, heavy, sticky	Steep, pressure-cook, bake, refry, braise	Bland	Add dry fruits and seasonings – good for infants and elderly

Temperature of Cooking Liquid/Grain	Texture	Compatible Cooking Methods	Flavor	Suggestions
COLD/COLD	Heavy, sticky	Dry-roast, sauté, soak, bake, boil, steep, pressure-cook, refry, braise, deep-fry		Good preparation for deep-fry and to be served with hot sauces
COLD/HOT	Light, sticky, drier, somewhat individual and chewy	Dry-roast, sauté, bake, steep, pressure-cook, refry, braise, marinate		Not extreme in texture. Serve with hot sauces or as a "pilaf"
HOT/COLD	Common, standard texture: neither heavy nor light	Soak, bake, boil, pressure-cook, refry, braise		Serve with a hot sauce. Can accommodate all kinds of serving styles
HOT/HOT	Light, fluffy, individual	Dry-roast, sauté, bake, boil, steep, pressure-cook, refry, braise, marinate		Put in soup or salads

It is important to consider the size of the vegetable you are placing in the grain. The size of decorative vegetables should be determined according to the size of the grain and the importance of the vegetable. Small diced vegetables will allow the grain to be the focus. Larger pieces of vegetables become the focus, making the grain the decoration. Imagine bright green seasoned broccoli with sprinkles of yellow millet, or marinated quinoa with sprinkles of sweet red pepper and parsley, or carrots and millet cooked together to form a golden orange combo. Whatever their size, cut vegetables into pieces of equal size for even cooking.

Although beans add protein to grain dishes, I rarely cook beans and grain together. Insuring that a bean is well cooked is somewhat tricky even without grain; cooking them together requires even more finesse. My preference is to cook them separately in first-stage methods and combine them in second-stage methods.

When beans and grain cook together in the first stage, beans need to be precooked. If pressure-cooking is the first-stage cooking method, cover the beans with water, boil them for at least 20 minutes until the water has totally reduced; then combine the beans, grain, and cooking liquid and cook according to the grain chart. If steeping the grain, make sure the beans are well cooked. Hard beans don't digest easily and can cause problems like flatulence and stomach cramps.

Cooking salt into beans helps the protein assimilate in bodies but only if used after the beans are already soft.

Measure the cooking liquid as if you are cooking just grain, but measure the grain and beans together before they are washed or soaked to determine the amount of cooking liquid. For example, 1½ cups of grain and ½ cup of beans equals 2 cups of grain. If rice is the chosen grain and the cooking method is steeping, after the beans are soft prepare the rice and beans with 4 cups of liquid. If pressure-cooking is the primary method, then 2 cups of combined rice and beans will need 3 cups of cooking liquid.

Seasoning

As cooks, we are responsible for drawing out the very best a food has to offer, so seasoning is a skill of great importance. For newcomers, it mostly takes courage. Knowing that seasonings are best when cooked into the dish or sauce makes the responsibility of the cook even greater. And then there is the unveiling, knowing that how you choose to season your dish reflects your personality. Are you cautious, flamboyant, delicate, sensual? What about your mood? Is it hot, sweet, bitter, indifferent? Notice your choices in seasonings and reflect on your frame of mind, or better, notice your mood and choose the seasonings to match or balance. Would a bitter frame of mind enjoy the sweetness of grain; would sour flavors soothe the moods? This observation is for fun, not intended to become another set of principles. Surprise yourself! Express yourself!

Herbs, spices, oils, vinegars, and salt are all seasoning agents. The value of learning to season grains and sauces while they are cooking is that salt and pepper aren't needed at the table when the cook seasons food properly. Seasonings become integrated into the dish at a point of transformation, making them more efficient and available for our bodies than if we dump them on top of the dish before eating it. When seasonings are added during cooking, the flavors have a better chance of integrating with each other and the food has a unified taste instead of a salt taste next to vinegar next to oil, etc.

Taste

Our taste buds can experience five main flavors: sweet, bitter, sour, pungent (hot), and salty. The art of seasoning is to find a balance between these tastes. For example, if a sauce is too bitter, we may add a sweet or salty ingredient. If food is too sour, we may need a salty, sweet, or pungent ingredient to offset the sourness. If it is too salty, we may find balance in a bitter or sweet flavor. Too pungent? Add a salty, bitter, or sweet ingredient. Learning which foods carry the different tastes will expand your ability to create new dishes and "fix" the ones that are not quite right.

We rely on our sense of taste and smell to determine how to season our dishes. Bitter flavors register in the taste buds at the back of the tongue; sweet flavors come through an area at the tip in front; sour flavors are sensed on the ridge of the tongue at the side; and salty flavors register near the front on the ridge. Two other tastes, one pungent and the other one, for lack of a better description, odd, are sensed in the general area of the tongue and walls of the mouth. Depending on the age and condition of each of us, these sensations may not register equally. Bitter and sour are usually strong and clear. Perception of salt depends on the saltiness of the individual's blood. Sweet is the most difficult of all to sense, which explains why sugar has become so important in the manufacturing of foods. Look at boxed cereals; most of them contain

CHART OF TASTES

	SWEET	SOUR	BITTER	PUNGENT	SALTY
GRAINS					
Buckwheat groats			X		
Oat groats	X				
Millet	X				
Quinoa			X		
Rice	X				
Sweet			X		
Basmati	X				
Wild			X		
Amaranth	X		X		
SALT SEASONINGS					
Sea salt					X
Vegetable salt					X
Miso	X				X
Tamari/Shoyu					X
Umeboshi		X			X
Sauerkraut		X			X
COOKING LIQUIDS					
Apple juice	X				
Orange juice	X				
Cranberry juice		X	X		
Lemon juice		X			
Vegetable stock	X				
Nut milk	X				
Beer			X		
Wine	X	X	X		
Sherry	X				
Mirin	X				
Vinegar		X			
Apple cider		X			
Rice		X			
Wine		X			
Umeboshi		X			X
Raspberry		X			

CHART OF TASTES (contd.)

	SWEET	SOUR	BITTER	PUNGENT	SALTY
HERBS & SPICES					
Arugula				X	
Basil	X				
Tarragon	X				
Bay leaf				X	
Fennel	X				
Mint				X	
Parsley			X		
Rosemary				X	
SPICES					
Allspice	X				
Caraway				X	
Cardamom	X				
Cayenne pepper				X	
Coriander	X				
Ginger (fresh)				X	
Garlic				X	
Horseradish				X	
Peppercorns				X	

some form of added sugar. As we practice chewing whole natural foods, our instincts for sweet taste will be revived, and "added sugar" will be difficult to take in.

Seasonings give more accurate readings if the food is not too hot or too cold. Our maximum taste sensitivity occurs in the range from 72 to 105°F (22 to 41°C), with sweet and sour sensations enhanced at the upper end, salty and bitter at the lower (Harold McGee, *On Food and Cooking*, pp. 568–569).

The taste chart on pages 23–24 outlines the taste character of various seasoning agents. You may find one ingredient carries two or more tastes. When in doubt about which seasoning to use, ask your right brain for ideas.

Smell and taste are closely related, with our smelling apparatus in even more direct line with the brain. As we sniff the scents of seasonings that have been released into vapors (when crushing herbs, for example),

TRADITIONAL FLAVOR COMBINATIONS

	MEDITERRANEAN	INDIA NORTH AFRICA MIDDLE EAST	LATIN AMERICA	ORIENT
OIL	olive	peanut sesame/tahini	corn	light sesame dark sesame
COOKING LIQUID	lemon juice wine vinegar wine	lemon juice	lime juice beer	sake mirin rice vinegar umeboshi
HERBS/SPICES	parsley oregano basil rosemary fennel thyme marjoram tarragon garlic	allspice cumin coriander ginger (dry) mint marjoram cinnamon turmeric saffron cilantro cardamom nutmeg	chilies sweet peppers oregano cilantro garlic	ginger (fresh) garlic cilantro (Chinese parsley) Chinese five spice mustard

messages usually enter the right side of the brain, where experience is recorded and appropriate selections are made. The throat and the nasal cavity are connected, making a pathway for the sense of taste to meet the sense of smell. Both the taste buds and the olfactory nerves have regenerative powers, which is good because they will tire if asked to discriminate between too many flavors at once.

Seasoning sauces and grain dishes is a challenge for the senses. Traditional and ethnic dishes dictate specific combinations of seasonings. Garlic, oregano or basil, and olive oil season many Italian dishes, and ginger, shoyu, mirin, and sesame oil are a common combination in Oriental dishes. The chart of traditional flavor combinations will show you patterns that have worked for centuries and provide a foundation for spontaneous cooking.

Serving Suggestions

In theory, how you present your grain dish has a great impact on how it is received. Although the recipes in this book are everyday, quick-cooking grain dishes and easy-to-make sauces, appropriate for breakfast, lunch, or dinner, their presentation can stand up to the best. Think of them as elegant dishes created with simple food.

The principles of shape and color make a dramatic contribution. The quantity of the serving along with the style of sauce and other kinds of food that go with the meal will also be considerations.

Shape is related to texture. Dry, individual grains can be served in shallow bowls and plates or sprinkled into soup or vegetable dishes. Moister grains can be pressed hot into a mold, like a cup or bowl, or once cooled can be formed by hand into the desired shape. If using a mold or bowl, wet or lightly oil it first so that the grain will come out of the mold easily when inverted.

Color elements include the natural colors of the grain, decorative vegetables, and sauces. Ivory-colored sweet rice speckled with gray-black wild rice is an example of a dish where the grains themselves provide the color accents. When combining various colors of grain, cook them separately (the colors bleed if they are cooked together) and mix them before serving or layer them in a mold.

Salt seasonings will have an impact on color. Umeboshi can turn light grains and sauces pink. Tamari, shoyu, and miso will add a brown color. If you want to keep the dish or sauce white, use sea salt to replace some of the colored miso or umeboshi.

Acid ingredients such as vinegar and lemon juice will change a brilliant green vegetable to a drab yellow-brown. If using these seasonings on a green vegetable, do so immediately before serving if it is important to maintain the color.

The quantity of a serving of whole grains depends on its position in the meal. In a soup or stew, ½ cup of raw grain may suffice for 4 to 6 servings; if the main course is a grain salad, allow 1 to 2 cups dry grain for 4 to 6 servings.

I have seen people love grain dishes to the point of danger. Overeating a health-giving food is counterproductive, so judge the serving size according to personal need. The more we chew, the less quantity we need to eat.

Eating Whole Grains

Whole grains radiate a sense of purity. They are clean, simple foods that receive the thoughts, feelings, and energy of the cook. Fitting this revered food into the daily hustle is not always easy. I cringe when I see people standing, leaning to one side, maybe against a wall, shoveling in food to fuel them through the next event. One day I realized there was a direct relationship between the amount of energy, love, and care that I gave to meal preparation and the amount of reverence with which it was eaten. Cheese and tortillas, a standard quickie, were snarffed down on the run, while fried rice or rice pilafs, also favorites, were enjoyed at the table, with conversation even.

Could these simple whole grains really demand this much attention? Whole grains have not been part of our diet for a long time. With the increase of foods that are sweet and fluffy, vegetables often frozen or overcooked, our eating apparatus has become wimpy. Americans hold the title for champion speed eaters.

The digestive process for whole grain begins in the mouth. As it mixes with saliva, the grain is broken down into a form that makes its nutrients available to our bodies. Chewing is essential if we want to be nourished by grain. Toast, chips, and other refined grain products demand little chewing from us, and we usually can get them to slide down the hatch after a few bites.

Chewing whole grains to liquid produces tremendous side effects. The enjoyment of eating is prolonged, taste and smell faculties are exercised, and the sweetness of the carbohydrate is released through chewing.

"I like freshness and simplicity. It is the highest grade of sophistication and the most difficult part of cooking. Yet shape is important to me; what goes on the plate should have the quality of a painting."

Gunter Seeger, chef at The Ritz Carlton Buckhead in Atlanta (Gourmet, December 1988)

When we eat whole grains, we eat less, and take more time to do it, slowing down to nourish ourselves, hopefully attaining a level closer to peace.

Condiments, Garnishes, and Design

Setting a table with form and style will make any food look good, and plain grains need as much presentation as they can get. Sauces, decorative vegetables, and condiments elevate the presentation of simple food to elegance. Mixing hot sauce into grain turns it into an everyday "casserole"; laying hot sauce generously beneath or over grain with garnishes of nuts, seeds, or decorative vegetables adds care and beauty to simple food.

Condiments are easily made from roasted nuts and seeds, roasted sea vegetables such as nori and dulse, relishes, pickles, and fruit and vegetable chutney.

To roast nuts in an oven, follow the oven dry-roasting method for grains (see pp. 67–68) but reduce the oven heat to 275–300°F. Nuts take much less time, about 7 to 10 minutes; the trick is to match the inside with the outside. Turn them frequently for even roasting and remove them immediately from the oven when the inside shade of a cut nut is a tone darker than a raw one. Many of the recipes call for tamari-roasted nuts; sprinkle the roasted nuts with undiluted tamari or shoyu directly in the baking pan, mix quickly, and remove from the pan. Let the nuts cool before slicing them for garnish. A variation for seasoning these delectable treats (often used as an appetizer) is to add a natural sweetener or mirin to the salt seasoning. Just a touch will do.

Nori and dulse also lend themselves to roasting. Their natural trace minerals contribute a salty flavor, and roasting dries them into a crumbly condiment. For variation, brush these sea vegetables with a mild combination of tamari and maple syrup or rice syrup; roast in the oven.

Garnishes: A sharp thin vegetable knife will shave vegetables ever so thin. Here are a few garnishing cuts that are quick and anyone can do them.

Placing Whole Grains in the Meal Plan

I do not recommend a diet of just whole grains; meals should include raw and cooked vegetables as well as proteins from various sources. A primary cooked grain with a luscious hot sauce could be the main dish of the meal, or it might be accompanied by a vegetable protein dish of tofu, tempeh, seitan, or beans, and a salad or cooked vegetable dish.

I don't want to prescribe another generic diet; my whole philosophy is based on instinct. With time and experience, you will know what and how much grain to eat and where and when to eat it during the day.

My personal experience has brought me to the following guidelines: If you eat dairy and animal foods but are concerned about fat and cholesterol, make whole grains and fresh and raw cooked vegetables the major part of the meal and reduce the amount of cheese and meat to a small portion of the total meal. If you are a vegetarian, vegetable proteins can amount to about 20 to 30 percent of a meal; surround them with whole grains, and fresh and raw cooked vegetables.

Ingredients

This chapter will introduce the qualities, character, and function of ingredients. Quality determines the success and healing power of your dish. Character reflects the way a food grows and how it performs in cooking. Knowing the function of food allows for greater creativity, understanding, and appreciation; it's a chance to create some intimacy between you and the food.

Grains

The following descriptions refer to the character of each grain without any pretreatment or seasoning. A general yield per cup of dry grain is given; however, yield can be affected by cooking methods and variations in the amount and kind of cooking liquid.

BUCKWHEAT

Buckwheat is a pseudograin belonging to the dock family. Aggressive, hardy, porous, and earthy, buckwheat grows well in adverse conditions; it thrives in locations where other crops fail, and will grow over any existing crop close by. The fruits (groats) are almost complete in the B vitamin line and carry strong portions of vitamin E. They are rich in the minerals phosphorus and potassium and are exceptionally high in iron and calcium.

Originally from the plains of China and Siberia, buckwheat is the basis of some of the most delicious whole-food dishes of Asia and Europe (piroshki, kasha varnishkas, and kasha knishes). Japanese cuisine treats buckwheat as a bread grain, mostly in the form of pasta (soba).

Buckwheat carries a strong earthy flavor, which people either love or hate. Raw groats are white with hints of green, gray, and tan. Roasted buckwheat (kasha) delivers a deep brown color and strong aroma. I almost always use it roasted rather than raw, but try it both ways and decide for yourself. Kasha is available both boxed and in bulk, but you will gain vitality by roasting the raw grain and storing it yourself.

The light angular shape of the whole buckwheat groat is distinctive. It is very porous, so it cooks quickly. Wash raw groats quickly and gently or they will drink the washing liquid, and you will have no control over the texture of your dish. Choose whole groats over broken grits.

Buckwheat loves the dry-roasting treatment, lots of oil, and any cooking method except boiling and pressure-cooking. Most sauces will work with buckwheat, but bean sauces may be too heavy, unless you make them very thin.

ENERGETICS:
Aggressive, quick, porous.
TEXTURE:
Dry, soft, light.
FLAVOR:
Hearty and earthy; bitter.
COMPATIBLE COOKING METHODS:
Dry-roast, sauté, bake, steep, braise, refry, deep-fry, marinate.
FAVORITE DISHES:
steeped or baked kasha, served with a hot sauce such as Creamy Horseradish or Mushroom-Onion (p. 161); braised with sauerkraut juice; croquettes.
NUTRITION:
E and B vitamins; calcium, iron, phosphorus, potassium.
YIELD:
1 dry = 4 cooked.

MILLET

The earliest recorded document about millet reports that it was a "holy plant" in China around 2800 B.C. As an ancient staple of India, Egypt, and North Africa, millet was once as important as wheat is today. One of the oldest North African strains was called "beard grass from Aleppo." Millet is still a major food source in Asia and North Africa. This tiny seed grows from a vertical cone-shaped head. The hulls have a dull shine, yellow-gold or red-brown in some varieties. They have terrific survival abilities, responding equally well in drought and water-logged conditions. Recognized as bird seed and cattle feed in Britain and the U.S., this grain has a long way to go to becoming a main dish on our tables.

Millet's energy is both rooted in the earth and abundant in flowers reaching to the heavens.

The people of Java grew millet as a border around rice to activate growth of the rice plant and encourage abundance. Its ability to transmit spiritual energy is recognized in the legends of many cultures. A key element in millet that might be directly related to its spiritual power is silica. This crystalline compound, also found in quartz crystals, is the element responsible for opening the plant to light and warmth.

With a nutritional profile of 5 percent fat (second only to oats in fat quantity), 10 percent protein, .05 percent sugar, 60 percent starch, 2.5 percent fiber, 2.8 percent minerals (a good supply of iron), and many of the B vitamins, you can see how millet has served as a major grain throughout history.

In choosing millet, look for bright yellow grains without any shiny hulls. (Give any hulls you get to the birds—they are not fun to eat.) Although it is a naturally dry grain, millet can be cooked to a creamy texture. Like that on oats and rice, the filmy layer that accompanies cooked millet is valuable nourishment. When cooked millet has cooled, it has an ideal texture for molding or shaping for refrying and deep-frying. Millet loves a sensual sauce, and can take any style of hot or cold sauce.

OATS

Like rice in Asia, wheat in the Mediterranean region, and quinoa in the Andes, oats played an important role in the early religions of northern Europe. Germanic priests celebrated the regenerative power of the grain in spring fertility rituals to the goddess Nertho. It's no coincidence that these rituals came at the same time of year that a lot of youths were "sowing their wild oats."

ENERGETICS:
Little compact seeds ready to release a megadose of food power, they can endure hardship and are extremely versatile.

TEXTURE:
Dry, soft.

FLAVOR:
Sweet.

COMPATIBLE COOKING METHODS:
Dry-roast, sauté, soak, boil, bake, steep, pressure-cook, braise, marinate, refry, and deep-fry.

FAVORITE DISHES:
Dry-roasted, boiled, and marinated; sautéed with vegetables and pressure-cooked; deep-fried.

NUTRITION:
Iron, potassium, calcium; B vitamins; protein.

YIELD:
1 dry = 3 cooked.

Oats were first discovered as a wild weed and mistaken for a mutant wheat berry. Their plants look different from other grains, as the seeds are housed in a double husk and hang downward from a podlike hull instead of spiraling upward like other grains. Nature protects this soft grain with a double hull, which may be the reason it is hard to find oat groats without hulls clinging to the grain. Although hulls are *true* fiber, they are most unpleasant and not meant to be chewed. Livestock thrive on oats, whether they are well cleaned or not. But as much as I prefer whole grains to those that are cut, I will choose steel-cut oats over whole oats if there are too many hulls clinging to the whole oat groats.

Oats thrive in the cold, wet sea climates of Britain, Scotland, northern Europe, and northwest America. They replaced millet in Europe following the Middle Ages, as people discovered increased physical strength and mental endurance from eating them. Easily digestible by young children, the elderly, and convalescents, oats took a leading role in the popular diet. Directly accountable to the metabolic system (digestive, reproductive), oats also provide natural antidepressant nutrients. Although oats have seven times the quantity of fat as rice, they are composed of chemical combinations that protect the heart, balance cholesterol, and help circulation. Thanks to one set of carbohydrates that changes to fructose and blends with insulin, oats have helped cure mild cases of diabetes (Udo Renzenbrink, *Die Sieben Getriede*). Fructose is a sugar occurring naturally in fruit. It is rare that I prepare any grain with fruit, but this explains why oats are the only grains I even consider cooking with fruit.

THE OAT BRAN SCAM. Today, oat bran has drawn great attention as a source of fiber. Fiber is certainly important; it creates enough volume in the intestines to stimulate the peristaltic responses that encourage natural elimination. But by separating and eating only the roughest part of the oat groat (bran), usually in an overreaction and an attempt to balance indulgence in other foods, we separate parts of the grain designed and balanced by nature to go together. Even though oat bran is soluble and fairly soft against the intestinal wall, I am concerned that too much bran will scrape the intestinal wall, creating more need for fat to soothe it.

When whole oats are cooked, they produce a milky lubricating film that coats the digestive tract and protects the intestinal wall. And in the whole grain the protein, fat, starch, and minerals are balanced with fiber. Besides, it seems wasteful ecologically to spend energy on separation rather than on the healing power of "the whole."

ENERGETICS:
Quick, smooth, and slippery. This fuel burns slowly in the body.

TEXTURE:
Creamy, soft, moist; whole groats are chewy.

FLAVOR:
Lightly earthy.

COMPATIBLE COOKING METHODS:
Dry-roast, sauté, soak; boil (whole), bake (all forms), steep (all forms), pressure-cook (whole); marinate.

FAVORITE DISHES:
Mr. Sanford's Breakfast Oats (p. 96); Baked Oats With Vegetables and Sage (p. 80).

NUTRITION:
Extremely high in protein, vitamins B and E, iron, calcium, and phosphorus.

YIELD:
1 cup dry = 2½ cups cooked.

The high (for grain) fat content of oats provides a soft, chewy, creamy, warming nourishment. To protect the fat from becoming rancid, oats contain a natural antioxidant. A dusting of oat flour can replace BHT as a preservative on fatty foods like chips, bacon, or nuts. Oats and wheat have similar protein content, but where wheat is high in gluten, oats are not.

You can find oats in three different forms: steel cut, steam cleaned and rolled, and whole groats (simply hulled, sometimes by steam). The cooking methods in this book work for all three forms, and although the bran and germ remain intact in each form, the energetic quality is different. Try them all.

Oats will respond to all cooking methods, but because of their high fat content, methods that involve oil should be used carefully. Deep-frying and refrying may not be as appetizing as sautéing. This is one grain (like barley) that goes well with rice. Cook oats and rice together in any cooking method. Oats are so very bland they need a great dose of herbs, spices, or vegetables.

QUINOA

Quinoa (pronounced keen-wa) is a pseudograin belonging to the Goosefoot family. This powerful food comes direct from the high plains of the Andes Mountains in South America, where it is nicknamed "the mother grain" for its life-giving properties.

According to Steve Gorad, the founding president of the Quinoa Corporation, "Quinoa was as important to the Incas as the buffalo was to the American Indian. They used the whole plant in daily life." The young plants, rich in minerals, supplied deep green leafy vegetables; the seed was staple nourishment; the stalks became fuel in that high-altitude location void of wood; and the ashes were mixed with the coca plant to increase its mind-altering effect. Each year in planting ceremonies, the Inca (ruler) would plant the first row of quinoa with a gold planting stick. The grain was also mixed with blood to form dolls for religious rituals.

This high-altitude grain thrives in thin, dry air and poor, sandy soil, under the strain of intense radiation from the sun at high altitudes and below-freezing temperatures. The power reflected in quinoa's physical endurance is matched in its nutritional value. The National Academy of Sciences has called it "one of the best sources of vegetable protein in the vegetable kingdom." The essential amino acid balance is close to the ideal set by the United Nations Food and Agriculture

Organization. It is a complete protein with a quality "equal to that of dried milk." Some varieties of quinoa have a very small floury section in the endosperm, but this constitutes less than one percent gluten, making quinoa a great alternative for people with wheat and corn allergies.

Now quinoa is being grown around the world. Like millet and rice, it varies tremendously, with more than 2,000 known varieties. In 1982 Steve Gorad traded an Andean farmer the shirt off his back for seed grain, and a Colorado quinoa growing program was launched under the supervision of Colorado State University. Seed has spread to other continents and a variety of climatic regions, testing the reproductive strength of this little pseudograin.

All quinoa are very small elliptical seeds, with an average circumference of 1/16 of an inch and varying slightly in thickness. Generally it has a dry, bitter character, and the color ranges from off-white to black. At this time, imported quinoa is an off-white plump kernel. Domestic quinoa is gray and slightly smaller, with a rich and glutinous character. Black quinoa is truly black with a hint of purple, very small, and not readily available. It is a delicacy like wild rice.

Quinoa is fast food. The light little seeds cook very quickly by any cooking method. As they cook, the germ (which is in the outside of the grain) unfolds, looking like a partial spiral. Some say this glistening translucent grain with its spirals resembles caviar when cooked.

Quinoa needs to be washed thoroughly. Nature surrounds the seeds with a protective coating called saponin to protect the seed from the high intensity of the altiplano sun; it's also extremely bitter, providing a natural repellent to insects and birds. Commonly quinoa is washed by hand; change the water frequently to remove the rust-colored saponin. Another method of insuring that the saponin has been removed is pearling, a mechanical process of buffing off the outermost edge of a kernel. Some of the small grains may bypass commercial cleaning, so you still need to wash it well to avoid bitterness. Even though quinoa is small, it won't slip through a strainer if the grain is wet and you pour it through slowly, letting the kernels rest on top of one another.

RICE

Originating in India, Southeast Asia, and China around 4000 B.C., this legendary grain is now the second most produced food in the world. It is found on tables of the rich and the poor, and placed on private altars and in temples for worship. Symbols of the rice plant are objects of art and the grains are showered on newlyweds as a fertility rite.

ENERGETICS:
Lightweight and strong with subtle powers of satisfaction.
TEXTURE:
Al dente to soft.
FLAVOR:
Bitter.
COMPATIBLE COOKING METHODS:
Dry-roast, soak, sauté, boil, bake, steep, pressure-cook, braise, marinate, refry, deep-fry.
FAVORITE DISHES:
Dry-roasted, boiled, and marinated; sautéed, steeped, served with hot nut sauce.
NUTRITION:
Complete protein, E and B vitamins, calcium, phosphorus, iron.
YIELD:
1 cup dry = 4 cups cooked.

"It seemed that when the god of gods, Izanagi, came down to earth and created the islands that became Japan, he also created a pantheon of lesser gods and goddesses. The god of the sea didn't fancy being wet all the time, so he came ashore, had a disagreement with the goddess of food, and slew her. From her buried corpse five plants at once sprang up — first the soybean, then a larger common bean, and following were rice, wheat, and barley."

Japanese legend
Quoted in
The New Yorker,
March 11, 1985

Rice is not as rooted in earth energy as other grains as it grows; instead it aspires to the cosmos. Rice has the most water content of all grains, linking it to the coolness of the moon, just as millet gathers warmth from the sun. This food nourishes the spirit in an unearthly manner. The water content of rice helps it act as a diuretic, guiding the flow of liquid through the tissues, assisting circulation, blood pressure, and the kidneys.

Unlike other grains that have a distinct texture and flavor, rice appears to be very plain. Being plain is its distinction and its virtue. Rice is so plain and humble that it makes itself available for any kind of dish. At the same time, by being so mild and of light character it becomes universal, not limited by texture or flavor. Rice is a blank canvas for the culinary artist; all compositions are possible with rice.

Rice grows in many parts of the world, including Italy, Spain, Asia, China, India, South America, Africa, Australia, and the United States of America, and it has adapted to the cooking styles of all these regions. Unlike other grains, it likes warm, moist growing conditions. There are thousands of varieties of rice. Most of them are polished, removing valuable bran that contains vitamins and minerals. Natural rice has a reputation as a great source of B vitamins.

You may use the cooking methods in this book with any variety of rice, but the information given pertains to whole, unprocessed brown rice in all its varieties: long, medium, short, sweet, basmati, wild, and specialty rices. I love to play with their different qualities, responding to the variety of energetics, flavors, and colors. Each kind of rice can be prepared with all the cooking methods, but the more you experience their individual characters the sooner you will develop cooking patterns for each kind of rice.

SHORT-GRAIN BROWN RICE. I can't say enough about this grain, one of the most important staples of natural food cooking. When you look at the grain with your right brain, it reveals its spiritual quality as a short, oval, semitranslucent kernel, off-white with traces of green. Green color in the raw kernel indicates freshness; green kernels hold equal or more nutritional value than brown rice. After cooking, it maintains a beige, off-white color.

MEDIUM-GRAIN BROWN RICE. This graceful grain is the largest of the brown rice varieties. The color and shape of medium-grain rice is similar to that of short-grain rice, but the kernels are bigger, longer, plumper, and sometimes stickier when cooked. The germ, which stands out as an opaque white spot against the translucent quality of the grain, is easy to see.

LONG-GRAIN BROWN RICE. The long, thin, translucent kernels of long-grain rice reveal spots of white and green when raw, and cook up almost white. Less plump, these kernels are a little drier and store less fire and water energy than the other brown rice varieties. This grain is a perfect choice for mixing with wild rice, baking a pilaf, or making fried rice. I choose this grain when I want to create an individual, semidry texture. It is also my first choice when playing with the color and cooking liquid.

SWEET BROWN RICE. This sticky grain is also known as glutinous rice. Glutinous refers to the gluelike consistency of the starch, not to the protein gluten. In fact, sweet rice contains very little gluten, although its protein content surpasses that of other rice. The kernels are the same length and color as short-grain brown rice, but sweet rice is fatter and opaque, not translucent. The misleading name needs clarification; the grains are slightly bitter, not sweet. Japanese custom serves sweet rice cakes for the New Year. Traditionally, sweet rice is hand pounded, but my love for this food outweighed my limited amount of extra energy and helped me devise a simple approach to making mochi (see p. 112).

BASMATI AND TEXMATI BROWN RICE. Basmati brown rice is an aromatic long-grain variety native to India and Pakistan. This is an extremely light and flavorful brown rice, with a delightful aroma even in its raw form. Indian rice dishes usually season the cooking liquid with spices such as cardamom, cinnamon, and cloves. Texmati rice is a domestic variety grown in Texas; another local variety called Calmati is grown in California. When cooked, this brown rice looks white.

SPECIALTY RICE. Lundberg Farms in Richvale, California, has brought a number of exciting varieties of rice to the market in the last fifteen years.

Mahogany is a short-grain variety named for its deep color.

Black japonica is a small short-grained variety with a rich black color. It is usually found in combination mixtures with other specialty rices. The bran in this grain is soluble, making the bran more usable and turning the cooking liquid purple.

Wehani is a long and plump variety originally from India, with a rich russet color and an especially strong aromatic flavor.

Royal is another full-flavored, aromatic long-grain variety.

ENERGETICS:
Radiant and pure.

TEXTURE:
Chewy or soft.

FLAVOR:
Sweet (most varieties); bitter (sweet brown rice); earthy (wild rice); aromatic (wehani, black japonica, royal, basmati).

COMPATIBLE COOKING METHODS:
Dry-roast, sauté, soak, boil, bake, steep, pressure-cook, braise, marinate, refry, deep-fry.

FAVORITE DISHES:
Pressure-cook and serve with hot sauce; pressure-cook, deep-fry; Lemon-Dill Rice (p. 79); croquettes.

NUTRITION:
B vitamins (thiamine, niacin); phosphorus, calcium, potassium.

YIELD:
1 cup dry = 2½ cups cooked.

Field run japonica is a blend of colors, like Indian corn, all grown together on one plant.

WILD RICE. Wild rice, a distant relative of the cultivated rice plant, is not a grain but an aquatic grass seed (*Zizania aquatica*). Harvested by hand by Native Americans, wild rice will always be limited in supply; its price reflects both its scarcity and the difficulty of harvest. The flavor of this grain is very strong, so a little used respectfully goes a long way. Wild rice has a greater concentration of B vitamins, magnesium, and zinc than rice and is one of the highest grains in protein content, but it remains one of the least explored as far as cooking potential. The very thin grains can be as long as one inch. As they cook, they open to show a soft white-gray inside against a curling brown-black cover.

SPECIAL GRAINS

The following grains are new to the commercial marketplace. They all have distinct characteristics. Not only are they as ancient as ancient can be, they have powerful nutritional profiles. Although confirmation is not 100 percent, the majority of people suffering from lupus and celiac-sprue illness can benefit from these low-gluten grains.

AMARANTH. Another ancient grain revisited, amaranth (*Amaranthus* spp.) carries a history similar to quinoa. Originally cultivated in the New World by the Aztecs, it was also known in ancient China, and today China is the major producer of this grain, followed by Mexico and Central America.

Amaranth is a member of the Pigweed family. It grows at low altitudes, and needs a wet seedbed to sprout followed by a dry growing season. Kansas and Nebraska offer the best growing conditions in North America, followed by Colorado and Wyoming, although the potential range extends from Pennsylvania to Arizona, the Dakotas, and the Canadian prairies.

With its nearly wild nature, amaranth gives farmers a few challenges. It doesn't necessarily grow in straight rows, and wild pigweed is commonly found among the plants (in fact, the extremely bitter black seeds frequently found in a supply of amaranth usually come from pigweed). Amaranth seeds will mold on the stalk with too much moisture, or fly away in the wind if the air is too dry. The six-foot seed stalks survive best when picked by hand. The plant has some growing advantages, however, including shallow roots just below the surface that crowd out most weeds, making chemical herbicides unnecessary.

Future farmers will most likely conquer the quirks of growing amaranth because this tiny grain is a nutritional powerhouse. Its protein content surpasses that of other grains, especially in the essential amino acid lysine. It is also high in vitamins C and A, and quite low in carbohydrates (for grain) and gluten. The leaves are also delicious cooked as a vegetable, and research is in progress on the use of the stalks for fiber.

Amaranth is commonly treated as a bread grain, ground into flour for use in breads, cereals, and pasta. In this book, it is used as an unusual dish grain. The itty-bitty seeds (so small that a pound may contain a quarter million) give off a loud crunch even when they are cooked. The cooked grains are coated with a thick, shiny film that makes them shimmer like caviar. And the flavor? It's intense. If the bitter flavors are subdued, a strong, earthy, and very sweet cornlike flavor comes through. My favorite way to achieve this is to steep the dry-roasted grain in beer, then smother it with a sauce or refry it with decorative vegetables. You can also combine it with rice for deep-frying. Marinating it is difficult at best.

JOB'S TEARS. Presently imported from Japan, this bead-shaped kernel of a tall grass (*Coix lacryma-jobi*) has been enjoyed in China for more than 4,000 years. Now Italy, Asia, Thailand, and the United States are awakening to this pleasant food. Legend hints of Native American tribes in Florida and Louisiana who found Job's tears growing among the grasses.

Named for the tearlike cluster of seeds that hang over the stalk, Job's tears are protected by hard, shiny, gray-beige hulls. Ornamental varieties produce kernels for bead work. The variety cultivated for food carries a good amount of protein, vitamin B1, and potassium.

Like big, elegant, luscious tears, these snow-white pearly beads provide a silky, moist, and slightly grainy texture. Coated in a light film of starch, this grain cooked whole is delicious served with a hot sauce, refried, or braised.

For more information on Job's tears, contact:
Eden Foods
701 Tecumseh Road
Clinton, Michigan 49236

TEFF. One of the tiniest seeds yet to be classified in the whole-grain category, teff (*Eragrostis tef*) is outstanding for its part in the history of its native Ethiopia, for its nutritional and physical attributes, and for its unusual, pleasant taste.

Imagine the survival of an unconquered civilization, one of the oldest on record, where the hero is the tiniest grain in the world. Surviving Greek and Roman culture, Ethiopia has never been changed by invasion as have other civilizations whose enemies would destroy the food supply to conquer. Because a whole year's supply of seed stock (about two pounds) could easily be carried into hiding, the Ethiopians could return to fields that had been burned, plant again, and harvest a new crop in 120 days.

In the rich language of Ethiopia, the word teff translates as "lost": lost because, being so tiny, it is easy to lose; lost because it can easily hide; and lost because, should water fall prematurely on the panicles of seed, the water-soluble bran will begin to decompose.

Although it is tricky to grow, teff is a drought-resistant, abundant food. One tiny seed of teff can produce as much food as a single grain of wheat. Best known for its calcium and mineral content, teff also carries valuable protein and soluble bran. Like oat bran, its water-soluble layers of bran are valuable in breaking down cholesterol.

Teff has more food value when the seed is open. Since it is difficult to chew this fine a grain, pretreatments are useful. Soaking, dry-roasting, and sautéing help prepare the outer layers of grain to open.

Teff is primarily a bread grain, used to make the staple Ethiopian flat bread *injera*. It is sweet in flavor, but with a strong character thanks to its intense mineral content. With a slight molasses taste and a gelatinous texture, this grain makes a good morning cereal.

White, red-purple, and brown varieties are available through the American grower Wayne Carlson. For information and special ordering, contact his company:

Maskal Teff
1318 Willow Street
Caldwell, Idaho 83605

STORING RAW GRAINS

Raw grain should be stored in airtight glass or ceramic jars.

Occasionally you may see grain clumped together in little balls that look like they have static cling. This condition is caused by grain moth eggs. The eggs will not harm you or your grain; just wash the grain well before preparing it. If you have a large quantity of grain in this condition, wash it all, dry-roast it, and store it. When eggs are present in grain, there is a chance that moths have hatched and the larvae have eaten the germ or other parts of the kernels. Be careful opening a bag or jar in which moths have hatched; if the moths fly out they quickly find a new home and multiply. Open and empty the grain outside in the garbage or compost.

STORING COOKED GRAINS

Cooked grains should be stored in the refrigerator only if they are cooked with vegetables, broth, or beans. Vegetables and beans spoil faster than grains and need the refrigeration, but refrigeration will dry out cooked whole grains, creating a hard, unfriendly texture. Remember that preparing grain in the first stage without vegetables or beans will give you more versatility for dishes as well as storage.

Grains prepared with only water and salt can be stored at room temperature up to three days in the winter and one day in the summer. Mold usually won't appear on the room-temperature grain for five days. If the grain turns slightly sour in storage but is not yet moldy, you can still use all the secondary cooking methods (except marinating) to prepare a delicious dish. If this sounds alarming, just remember that the ingredients are identical to those in sourdough bread: grain, salt, water, and time.

Cooking Liquids

Think of cooking liquid as "liquid" and not simply water and you can go wild with new dish creations. Of course, water is the most common cooking liquid, but other liquids, including stock, nut milk, juice, beer, wine, and vinegar, can replace some or all of the water in first-stage cooking methods (boiling, baking, steeping, and pressure-cooking) and second-stage braising liquids and marinades. The liquid ratios on the grain chart consider water as the cooking liquid.

WATER

Quality water is essential for health, and matches the goodness of simple foods, but it takes effort to find a source of good water for daily cooking and drinking. When I started cooking with natural foods, I would go to a local well and pump five-gallon bottles full of well water. Later I had spring water delivered weekly. I won't pretend to be an expert on water. I do know that there are choices to make about it. If you have no idea where to begin your search, inquire at the local health food store or with a naturopathic doctor.

The advantage of choosing water as the cooking liquid is that the grain will be more available for second-stage cooking methods. With no added flavors, all options remain open, and there are no added ingredients that might lead to premature spoiling. Water is fast and easy and gives a clear, clean feeling to the grain dish.

The next step up in complexity from plain water is flavored or colored water. A small amount of fresh ginger, garlic, whole peppercorns, cinnamon stick, cloves, saffron, or cardamom will delicately flavor a simple grain cooked with water. (Remove the sticks, pods, and pieces of spice before serving.) To be really outrageous, use a few pinches of turmeric, paprika, or beet juice to color a dish beautifully.

STOCK

Stocks are a great choice of cooking liquid, especially for sauces. Chicken, beef, and vegetable stock work equally well in preparing grain dishes and sauces. However, unless skimmed, meat stocks will add fat, so you won't need to use a vegetable source of fat. Vegetable stocks feel very clean and free from any fat or oil content. Unless you want a pink, green, or orange-colored dish, be careful of the vegetables you choose to create the stock. Light-colored vegetables are recommended.

Vegetable stock can be stored in the refrigerator for up to a week. It is better to use fresh vegetables and store the stock than to try to get anything out of a vegetable that has been waiting in the refrigerator for several days.

Kombu contains a natural form of MSG (monosodium glutamate) that draws out the best a food has to offer. It is so full of minerals and nourishment that kombu and water alone can make a vegetable stock.

NUT MILK

Nut milk is a homogenized liquid made by blending raw nuts with water until the fiber is completely broken down; it is an excellent substitute for dairy cream or milk. It won't be exactly like dairy milk, but if you are avoiding dairy food for any reason, you will be thrilled to see what nut milk can do. Unlike dairy milk, nut milk is light and clean feeling, not thick and mucousy. I have used various nut milks as substitutes for dairy hundreds of times; grain dishes cooked with nut milk are luscious, heavy, and creamy. I strongly suggest you serve them fresh and hot, as they change when the oil cools off.

Some nuts have a higher oil content than others. Chestnuts and filberts are at the low end of the spectrum; macadamias and cashews are at the high end. Pecans, almonds, and peanuts are somewhere in

MAKING VEGETABLE STOCK

MAJOR VEGETABLES	MINOR VEGETABLES	HERBS & SPICES
kombu	carrots	parsley
cauliflower	cabbage	basil
(include leaves)	kale	thyme
leeks	burdock	rosemary
shallot	rutabaga	lemon grass
fennel	winter squash	turmeric
summer squash	parsnip	paprika
celery		tarragon
mushrooms		marjoram
		dill
(whole grain)		garlic
(noodles)		ginger

MAJOR VEGETABLES may be used alone or in combination but must be the largest amount of the vegetables chosen to create a broth.

MINOR VEGETABLES may be used singly or in combination only in small quantities with a group of major vegetables.

HERBS AND SPICES – there are many others to choose from; look at the Foods to Have on Hand chart on pages 12-16.

STEPS FOR CREATING A VEGETABLE STOCK

1. Fill pot with cold water
2. Clean and cut vegetables into large pieces; put in water.
3. Rinse herbs and put in pot with a pinch of sea salt.
4. Bring to a boil; gently boil for 20 minutes.
5. Strain; store in refrigerator for up to one week.

the middle. Sesame, pumpkin, and sunflower seeds can also be used to create a milklike product.

To make nut milk as a cooking liquid for grain cookery, blend five to eight parts water with one part whole raw nuts or seeds in a blender. If using a food processor, first chop the nuts to a paste. Slowly add cooking liquid (water, wine, or juice) through the feed tube until it is blended with the nut paste and foaming. Another way to make nut milks is to blend liquids with nut butters (roasted nuts or seeds ground to a paste). I prefer raw nuts (or raw nut butters) when making nut milk for cooking grains in the first stage; either roasted or raw works fine for sauces. Roasted nuts yield a darker dish.

Because nut milk contains a lot of oil and the grain chart is geared for water as the cooking liquid, use one-fourth more nut milk per cup of dry grain to allow for the oil.

FRUIT JUICE

When used in combination with water, fruit juice sweetens a dish slightly, but not too much for main-course dining. When fruit juice provides all of the cooking liquid, it makes the dish a dessert. Juice produces a heavier texture as well as great sweetness. There will be a reduction in volume of grain when cooking with juice.

When using fruit juice for sauces, remember that fruit and nuts go well together. Because sauces almost always require an oil, choose a nut or seed oil (filbert oil or sesame seed oil, for example) to go with the juice. Fruit juice as a cooking liquid is especially wonderful in cold sauces. Fresh orange, lemon, and pineapple really come through. Cranberry, apple, pineapple, and orange juices are all worth exploring.

WINE, BEER, AND MIRIN

These strong cooking liquids are rarely used alone but are most successful in combination with other liquids such as water, stock, or nut milk. Red wines change light sauces and grains to purple. When selecting wine to cook with, do so as if you were serving an elegant meal. In other words, don't buy cheap wine, because the quality comes through in the cooking just as much if not more than in the drinking. Sake and chardonnay are two favorite white varieties.

Beer deserves a place as a cooking liquid for grain. Its slightly bitter dimension can be used to accent the same flavor in grains, or to match a strong-flavored grain like amaranth, teff, or quinoa. I prefer light beers as cooking liquid for first-stage methods, but darker beer and ale could accent any kind of sauce.

Mirin is a special sweet rice wine with a low alcohol content. Made from sweet rice, this is a fermented liquid, sticky by nature, and offers a distinctly Oriental flavor. Substitute or alternate with sherry or other kinds of wine. My favorite use for mirin in grain cookery is for cold sauces, refrying, and braising.

VINEGARS

I use a variety of vinegars for seasoning braising liquids and cold sauces. The function of this sour ingredient is first to "cut through" the taste and second to dilute the substance of a dish or sauce. Balancing both oil and salt, this kind of flavor used in small quantities can be the secret element that makes a successful dish. It can also stimulate digestion.

Vinegars are natural by-products from the fermentation of a variety of foods, including rice, barley, apples, grapes, and plums. A secondary fermentation converts the alcohol produced by yeast fermentation into acetic acid. Different vinegars represent different cultural traditions: rice and plum vinegars bring an Oriental flavor; wine vinegars (white, red, and herb- or spice-flavored) impart a taste of the Mediterranean; cider vinegar has always been part of American cuisine; and malt vinegar of British. Stocking two or three different kinds of vinegar will give more dimension to your cooking repertoire and will begin to give you options other than the traditional uses for these delightful seasoning agents.

Fruit vinegars require a higher acetic acid level than grain vinegars to stabilize the fermentation. (An exception is umeboshi plum vinegar, which is also cured with salt.) Distilled vinegar is much stronger than wine vinegar in its acid content. It doesn't appeal to me as it seems void of any delicious flavors or energetic qualities.

APPLE CIDER VINEGAR. This has a rich amber color. The acetic acid level is a minimum of 4 percent. Apple cider vinegar has a sweet, light flavor in addition to sour, so it is fairly neutral and can be used for almost any occasion. Sweet and sour sauce is one place apple cider vinegar shines.

MALT VINEGAR. This has a deep brown color with a hint of amber and a light flavor; its acetic acid level is at least 4 percent. Used on "fish & chips" in Britain and in pickled walnuts, this is a delicious light vinegar that could work for any dish. Braising liquids for grain love malt vinegar.

BROWN RICE VINEGARS. These are also low in acid content. Their auburn color can range from light to deep brown; the darker the color the stronger and more fragrant the vinegar. Famous in Oriental-style dishes, this seasoning likes to be with grain more than most fruit-based vinegars.

WINE VINEGARS. These are generally stronger than grain-based vinegars, at about 6 percent acetic acid. The deeper the color the stronger the flavor. Mediterranean sauces like vinaigrette, mayonnaise, and

COOKING LIQUIDS

LIQUID	ENERGETICS	TEXTURE	FUNCTION	FLAVOR	COMPATIBLE COOKING METHODS	FAVORITE
Water	Pure clean, simple	Smooth	Substance	Neutral	All	Colored; flavored
Vegetable Stock	Earthy	Smooth	Substance	Mineral rich	All	Kombu cauliflower; onion; fennel
Nut Milk	Light, milky	Dense & chewy for grain dishes; creamy for hot sauces	Substance	That of the seed or nut butter	Bake Steep	First-stage methods and hot sauces
Fruit Juice	Heavy for grain dishes; light for hot & cold sauces	Sticky	Substance & accent	Sweet	All first-stage and second-stage except refry and deep-fry	Steeped grain; nut butter & clear sauce; cold sauces
Vinegar	Cutting through & expanding	Clear	Accent	Sour, fermented	Second-stage cooking methods & hot and cold sauces	Marinades & braising liquids
Mirin	Delicate	Slightly thick	Accent	Exotic, sweet	All	Braising liquids; hot sauces; cold sauces
Beer/Wine	Strong	Color	Accent	Fermented	All	

hollandaise are the traditional uses for this kind of vinegar, but in grain cookery we cross traditional culinary borders. Even though I use wine vinegars most frequently with herbs such as basil, tarragon, fennel, or thyme, I have been surprised by cross-cultural combinations of wine vinegar with miso or tamari. Balsamic vinegar is a special wine vinegar from Italy with a deep flavor and a touch of sweetness.

FLAVORED VINEGARS. These are created with herbs or spices. They are easily made by heating the vinegar (cider, white rice, or wine) almost to the boiling point and pouring it into a glass bottle with herbs and spices. Let it cure for about ten days in a warm sunlit place, then taste. Strain when it reaches the desired strength. Use for marinades and braising liquids.

UMEBOSHI VINEGAR. This will be love at first taste. My all-time favorite seasoning, this is both a salt seasoning and a vinegar. Made from Japanese plums or apricots, sea salt, and beefsteak leaves (*shiso*), it has a glorious pink color and a strong salty and sour taste. It not only "cuts through," it adds salt. This seasoning is intense; in the past it was exclusively samurai food. Umeboshi vinegar is great as a braising liquid, or as an element of cold sauces. It can also supply the salt in first-stage grain cookery methods and replace tamari in refried dishes.

Salt and Salt Seasonings

Even though my name is Saltzman, I surprise myself at how strongly I feel about this miraculous element that brings the natural qualities of food to their very best expression. With time, liquid, and heat, this seasoning transforms a plain dish or a group of isolated tastes into a sweet harmony of flavors. At a time when diet-conscious people are reacting to an overconsumption of salt, I feel a need to reestablish a place for this highly regarded element. When used not in excess, but with quality, prudence, and purpose, salt will enhance the flavor of grain and prevent its premature fermentation.

I feel strongly that people have overreacted to salt, going from unconscious overindulgence to indiscriminate rejection. Poor quality salt (iodized salt with cornstarch, sugar, and free-flowing agents) is abundant in processed foods. Along with the natural sodium compounds found in meat and dairy products, all this salt has stressed the nation's ability to handle salt. These compounds are dangerous in the volumes that infiltrate prepared foods, but the saddest part to me is that people have dulled their ability to taste and enjoy natural flavors. In response to this

"Salt is an ancient food. It has always been one of the basic raw materials of life itself. Life arose in the sea perhaps three billion years ago, and it stayed in the sea until only about four hundred million years ago. Our blood, our tears, and most of the other juices of life within us have approximately the same salt content as the sea had when our remote ancestors left it to begin living in fresh-water rivers and on the land."

Robert Froman
The Science of Salt

chain of events, people are told, "Don't eat salt," so they eliminate it from cooking, but continue to find it in processed foods.

The only ingredients in this book that contain salt are straight salt and salt seasonings. We chose them consciously, with prudence and purpose. You can eliminate salt for a while to balance an oversalted system, but when you don't eat highly processed foods, meat, or dairy products, salt will become an essential ingredient for your sanity.

The function of salt is to assist the natural flavors of food to travel in and among themselves through their cell walls, bringing harmony to a dish. All first-stage cooking methods require a pinch of sea salt. With the exception of its occasional use in marinades, straight salt is always cooked into food. I think of the cook as a master of salt. When salt is used in the cooking process, food tastes better, and health is not at risk since the salt is transformed with fire and water. No salt is needed at the table when the cook takes responsibility for making food taste good. Salt seasonings are combinations of food, water, salt, and time. Miso, tamari, umeboshi, sauerkraut, and olives are salt seasonings. They can all perform the function of salt.

SEA SALT

There are many kinds of salt to choose from in the natural food marketplace. One basic choice is between land and sea salt. I prefer sea salt because it contains minerals and trace minerals that aren't available in earth; and since our food is grown in earth, it makes sense to me to gather what we can from the sea. If Mr. Froman is correct, and we do come from the sea, the nutrients in sea salt are valuable to us.

A little bit of this magical seasoning goes a long way. The salt I like to use is a natural, lumpy type made from sun-dried seawater. It doesn't flow from the salt shaker, but then pinching the salt between your fingertips is a great way to feel the quantity you are using. If it isn't the right amount, you will most likely never make the same mistake, as your body and your right brain will remember how much you used. Sea salt is two to three times more salty than other salts. The purer the salt, the saltier it is. Sun-dried sea salt attracts moisture, so keep it in a sealed glass jar, with a large enough opening for your hand to reach in for a pinch.

SALT SEASONINGS

Expanding the concept of salt to include salty seasonings such as miso, tamari, shoyu, umeboshi, and even olives and sauerkraut can give much more inventiveness to your cooking. Most of these salt seasonings have extra power, not just seasoning power; because they have undergone a fermentation process, beneficial enzymes are part of their essence.

MISO. This is a traditional Oriental bean paste. The primary ingredients are water, soybeans, salt, a fermented rice called *koji,* and some sort of grain (barley, rice, or buckwheat). People who are sensitive to soy products can look for miso made with other beans. Chickpeaso, made from chick-peas, is delicious and similar to white soy miso. The tremendous variety of miso reminds me of the variety of available bread and wine. Some are light in color and mild tasting while others are very dark and strong flavored. The lighter the miso, the sweeter and less salty it will be.

Because miso is a paste, it needs to be diluted with cooking liquid. A general amount to use per person is somewhere between 1 teaspoon and 1 tablespoon of undiluted miso in one cup of liquid. Try not to let miso boil; too much heat kills the beneficial bacteria and destroys the beneficial enzymes, though not the flavor.

Sometimes miso has white spots growing on it. This is not harmful or a sign of spoilage; it simply proves that miso is alive. Miso will keep a very long time (if covered), so you should never have to throw it out. If miso becomes hard and dry, moisten it with a little oil.

In grain cookery, my favorite use of miso is in hot and cold sauces and an occasional braising liquid.

TAMARI AND SHOYU. These are two types of naturally brewed soy sauce. Like a fine wine, the character of this salt seasoning is dependent on the quality and combination of ingredients and the skill of the brewing master. Tamari and shoyu are by-products of miso. As the fermented combination of grain, water, and beans ages, a liquid extract forms a puddle at the top of the miso keg. This liquid is called shoyu if wheat is used, tamari if wheat is not used. Each brand has a unique flavor; experiment with all of them. Soon you will develop a taste for tamari and shoyu as some people have developed a discriminating taste for wine.

Tamari and shoyu are primarily used in second-stage cooking methods. Diluted with cooking liquids or combined with vinegars or oils, these salt seasonings make delightful cold sauces, braising liquids, and marinades. A dash of tamari or shoyu can be the perfect finishing touch to a sauce or a refried grain dish. They do not need to be refrigerated.

"Salt is what makes things taste bad when it isn't in them."

Anonymous

UMEBOSHI PICKLED PLUMS. These come to us from Japan. Made from either whole apricots or Japanese plums, beefsteak leaf (*shiso*), and sea salt, this pickle is fermented for at least eighteen months. The beauty of this seasoning is that it is both salty and sour, and its color is a vibrant pink.

It comes in three forms: whole plums, paste, and vinegar. Whole plums may be used by pinching off a piece, or mashing the meat of the fruit. These are fairly salty; to reduce the impact of the saltiness and create a flavorful liquid, cover them with water and let them soak until needed. Whole plums need no refrigeration, but the liquid will need to be refrigerated. The stone of the fruit will give flavor to the soaking water or cooking liquid. (I like to suck on one and enjoy the flavor and feel my digestive enzymes activate.)

Umeboshi paste is the meat of the whole pitted plum, mashed into an easily usable paste. Like miso paste, it needs to be diluted for even distribution. Umeboshi paste is not as strongly flavored as whole plums packed in beefsteak leaves.

Umeboshi vinegar is the strongest of the three forms of this salt seasoning. Just as the liquid from the miso process forms tamari, the extracted juices from the combination of salt and plums create umeboshi vinegar.

This seasoning is my secret ingredient for many dishes. The salty and sour taste makes it a natural choice for braising liquids, marinades, and hot and cold sauces. It helps to cut through foods cooked in a generous amount of oil and adds a delightfully unique taste.

SAUERKRAUT. Either the cabbage or the juice can be used as a salt seasoning. Again, this fermented food is beneficial in aiding the digestion of grains. The combination of sour and salty is similar to umeboshi, but sauerkraut is both milder in strength and more distinct in flavor. Look for a natural sauerkraut, made with only salt and cabbage. Some brands even boast the use of organic cabbage and sea salt. Others are made without salt; obviously these won't work as a salt seasoning.

OLIVES. These provide both oil and salt seasoning. The meat of the green or black olive can be crushed to a paste and used like umeboshi paste. This is most effective with ripe black Greek-style olives. Olives are a great base for cold and hot sauces, and they provide decoration to whole-grain dishes.

VEGETABLE SALT. Although this product is loaded with dehydrated vegetables, its main ingredient is salt. Vegetable salt is very salty

SALT SEASONINGS

SALT SEASONING	ENERGETICS	TEXTURE	FLAVOR	COMPATIBLE COOKING METHODS	FAVORITE
Sea Salt	Crystalline in purity, holding richness of the sea	Hard, lumpy; not free flowing	Salty (twice the strength of table salt)	All except deep-fry	First-stage cooking methods; white flour sauce
Vegetable Salt	Mineral rich	Granular	Salty with vegetables	All except deep-fry	First-stage cooking methods; hot & cold sauces
Miso	Like moist earth	Paste	Mild–rich; sweet–salty; Fermented like wine	Second-stage cooking methods except deep-fry; hot and cold sauces	Braising; nut sauces
Tamari/Shoyu	Like liquid onyx	Thick or thin liquid	Salty; fragrant wine	All except deep-fry	Refry; Braising; Clear sauce; Cold sauce
Umeboshi	Brilliant, vital, charging	Paste or liquid	Sour & salty	All except deep-fry	Braise; marinate; nut sauce; cold sauce
Sauerkraut	Light, like an angel of the earth but cutting	Shredded or juice	Sour	Second-stage methods except deep-fry; sauces	Braising
Olives	Tight wads of power	Meaty paste		Sauces	Hot & cold sauces

but adds flavors like that of a bouillon mix without the oil. Because this is mostly salt, it is best to cook this flavored salt into the food, or dilute and mix it well in the liquid of a cold sauce; don't sprinkle it directly on cooked food.

Oils

Oil is essential for seasoning grains. Not only does it add flavor, it binds the substances and carries other seasoning agents evenly throughout the dish. The quality of the oil you use is very important. When we eliminate animal and dairy foods, vegetable oil becomes the main source of fat. There are many different kinds of vegetable oil to choose from and although all may be marked "natural" or "cold pressed" the best quality will be labeled "unrefined expeller pressed." There are many more oils in the market than the ones described here; the following vegetable oils are my choices of those worthy to cook with. All are polyunsaturated or monounsaturated, and high in vitamin E.

Oil is more than a lubricant; it has incredible variety of flavor, substance, and color. The oil you choose for your dish can be the significant ingredient that makes the dish sensational. The true test for quality comes from your experience of the oil. Does it radiate the flavor, the smell, and the color of the food it is supposed to be from?

Because oils impart the flavor of the food they come from and have different sensitivities to heat, they may be limited in how they are used. For example, walnut oil becomes very bitter when heated, so it is better for cold sauces. Any expeller-pressed oil other than safflower will not become hot enough to reach the temperature necessary for deep-frying. I try not to combine oils, as the simplicity and clarity of this style of cooking is what I like about it. But you could experiment. You can use canola oil as you would safflower oil but because it has little energetic quality or character, I don't use it.

Store oil in a cool or refrigerated place. Olive, peanut, and sometimes sesame oil will become cloudy and firm in the refrigerator. Little oil dispensers are useful if you cook with these oils frequently, because you can store the main supply in the refrigerator and have a small amount at hand ready to use.

CORN OIL. Unrefined expeller-pressed corn oil vitally represents yellow corn. It is thick and rich in substance, giving off an aroma of fresh corn and a glow of the golden sun. It is compatible with sautéed, baked, pressure-cooked, steeped, braised, and refried grain dishes. As it is a rich, heavy oil, I sometimes cook with it in place of butter and I rarely choose it for cold sauces.

OLIVE OIL. The difference in quality among olive oils is immediately obvious. Extra virgin olive oil is expeller pressed from the first pressing of the best quality olives; deep green in color, it emanates the delightful fragrance of olives. Virgin olive oil, from the second pressing of the olives, is lighter in color and flavor. The other form of olive oil (typically labeled "pure olive oil") has an almost yellow tint, a light substance, and no flavor at all. Although this is the form of olive oil that is suggested for high temperature cooking, it has been highly refined and is often a product of damaged olives. I prefer to use extra virgin for all the cooking methods in which I use olive oil: sauté, bake, steep, pressure-cook, marinate, braise, and refry.

Consider using the whole olive as a source for oil. Mash the meat into a paste and use it as a base for cold or hot sauces. This works best with olives that have soft meat.

PEANUT OIL. This can receive a high heat and still maintain its flavor. But unlike refined peanut oil that is frequently used for deep-frying, under high heat unrefined expeller-pressed peanut oil will continue to expand into a possible overflow and not reach the temperature necessary for deep-frying. It is great for sautéing, braising, refrying, and hot and cold sauces.

WALNUT OIL. This is a delicate, light-colored specialty oil. Its best use is in cold sauces; the slight bitterness that comes about when heating it can, in moderation, be a pleasant taste.

HAZELNUT OIL. This is my favorite nut oil. It is more versatile than the other specialty oils, almond and walnut. But more than its versatility, I like its deep, rich, light aroma and substance. Hazelnut oil has such a delicious flavor that it will guarantee a successful grain dish whether you sauté, braise, refry, use for marinade in a cold sauce, or prepare a hot sauce.

SESAME OILS. These can be light or dark. Dark sesame oil comes from roasted sesame seeds, is rich and deep brown in color, and imparts the most outrageous fragrance of any oil. Light sesame oil is pressed from raw sesame seeds; it has a strong yellow tint and a mild but clear sesame flavor.

SUNFLOWER OIL. This is my least favorite oil. It is very light in color and substance, but it carries a mild flavor that falls into the "odd" category. It is not bitter or pungent, but has some other taste that affects me the same way as hearing fingernails on a blackboard.

Especially when heated, this oil emits an odd flavor, one that I don't care for, but I see many people using sunflower oil, so they must like it. Either that or they aren't using a pure enough quality to recognize the taste. To be safe, use this oil in cold sauces only.

SAFFLOWER OIL. This is the most versatile of the unrefined oils. Its mild flavor allows it to go anywhere, and its ability to accept a high temperature without bubbling over makes it the perfect choice for deep-frying.

AVOCADO OIL. This is light in flavor and taste. Reading that this oil is usually made from damaged avocado fruit confirmed my instincts to use the whole avocado instead as an oil-based pulp. Mash it and use it as a thin paste that represents oil, especially in cold sauces.

GHEE (Indian-style clarified butter). This is the oil derived from butter. It's a health-giving and versatile oil, even for those on dairy-free diets, as all the milk solids are separated from the oil and discarded. To make ghee, warm unsalted butter to the slow boiling point until it foams; remove from the heat and let it sit until the milk solids fall to the bottom of the pan. Pour off the clear oil and store it in glass or ceramic jars, refrigerated or at room temperature. If you like this oil, keep some near the stove for easy use. As it is partially saturated, ghee is firm when cold, and it is easier to use at room temperature. I use it for refrying and for brushing filo dough.

FLAVORED OILS. These are made by infusing a light-flavored oil with herbs or spices. To make your own, place one to three kinds of herbs and/or spices in a bottle with the oil and set it in a dark place to cure for ten days. (Joseph, one of my cooking students, tells me his Italian grandmother stores cloves of garlic in a jar of olive oil in the refrigerator, which both preserves the garlic and flavors the oil.) After the curing period, remove the flavoring ingredient and store the oil in the refrigerator. Here are three variations to get you started.

Garlic oil: Place fresh peeled whole garlic cloves in olive, safflower, or sesame oil. Use this oil in cold and hot sauces or for sautéing, braising, and refrying.

Spicy oil: Place whole peppercorns or hot chili peppers, fresh ginger, coriander, cloves, etc. in corn, safflower, peanut, light sesame, or olive oil. Probably best for brushing on fish or cooking with beans, seitan, and other vegetable proteins.

Herbal oil: Place one to three kinds of herbs in oil. Rub fresh herbs (or crush dry herbs) first to release their fragrance. Tarragon, basil, thyme, and oregano are good choices in herbs; olive, light sesame, and safflower are suitable oils. Use these oils in sautéing, braising, marinating, and cold or hot sauces.

NUT AND SEED BUTTERS

In grain cookery, nuts and seeds and their butters can take the place of oil in the preparation of hot and cold sauces. When you think of them as oil, new creations are possible.

Nut and seed butters are made from roasted or raw nuts and seeds. Roasted seeds have more flavor than raw, as the oil is drawn to the outer surface. When the seeds are crushed and made into paste the oil is released, making it available to use as an oil. It may be easier to make your own nut butters than to find exotic ones in the stores. To make nut butter in a food processor simply chop roasted or raw nuts to a fine paste. Some nuts that are low in natural oil content will require additional oil during the grinding process.

PEANUT BUTTER. The most common of all nut butters, this makes an excellent binding agent for hot or cold sauces. Crunchy and smooth butters create a variety of textures. Because peanut butter is made from roasted peanuts, the sauce will be tan in color and its strong taste will permeate the entire dish. Whole roasted nuts can be added as a garnish or for texture in sauces.

ALMOND BUTTER. Unlike peanut butter, this can be made from raw or roasted nuts. The roasted variety is rich in flavor and has a deep brown color. Raw almond butter is a good choice for lighter colored sauces; its milder flavor blends more subtly with other ingredients. Almond butter usually leaves a trace of nutty pieces and gives a light texture to the dish.

CASHEW BUTTER. This has a high fat content, making it one of the creamiest and smoothest of all nut butters. Raw cashew butter, very light in color and mild in taste, is an ideal substitute for cream or milk. (I use it to make "white sauce.") Roasted cashew butter has a light brown color and a more dominant rich nutty flavor.

FILBERT (HAZELNUT) BUTTER. This is incredibly fragrant and light in flavor. It is lower in fat content and therefore less creamy than the other nut butters, but its flakes add a pleasant bit of texture.

PECAN AND MACADAMIA BUTTERS. These are less common, but the richness of their oil content makes them great possibilities as a source of oil. Their distinctive flavors make unusual, delightful dishes.

PINE NUT BUTTER. This is made from the kernel of the stone pine seed. It is high in fat, does not need to be roasted, and has a light

OIL CHART

OIL	ENERGETICS	COLOR	FLAVOR	COMPATIBLE COOKING METHODS	FAVORITE
Ghee	Rich, light	Transparent yellow	Butter	Refry, sauté, deep-fry	Refry; sauté
Corn	Rich, heavy	Bright yellow-gold	Corn	All except deep-fry	Refry; sauté; flour sauce
Hazelnut	Light	Yellow	Delicate hazelnut	All except deep-fry	Sauté; vegetable & flour sauce; cold sauce
Peanut	Medium weight	Rich yellow to brown	Fragrance of peanut	All except deep-fry	Sauté; vegetable & flour sauce; refry
Olive	Opulent	Green	Fruity	All except deep-fry	Braise; cold sauce
Safflower	Versatile	Light yellow	Neutral	All	Deep-fry
Sesame (Light)	Balanced	Light golden yellow	Sesame seeds	All except deep-fry	Refry; flour sauce
Sesame (Dark)	Potent	Dark amber-brown	Toasted sesame seeds	All except deep-fry	Refry; cold sauce
Sunflower	Weird	Pale yellow	Odd	Marinate	Cold sauce
Walnut	Wispy	Clear	Bitter	Marinate	Cold sauce

flavor. Used traditionally in *pesto,* this nut butter works well in both hot and cold sauces.

PISTACHIO NUT BUTTER. This offers a green tint to a sauce. Unless you are making a hot sauce where the nut butter will get to cook a bit, roast raw pistachios slightly or use roasted nuts to bring a balanced flavor to the dish. The color of this paste is greenish brown, and it has a rich, rewarding flavor.

SESAME SEED BUTTER. This is made from roasted whole sesame seeds. It is rich in flavor and pasty in substance. Its most frequent use is as a sandwich spread, but try it in your hot sauces.

SESAME TAHINI. This is made by grinding raw whole or skinned sesame seeds. There are many brands of this traditional Middle Eastern product, some of purer quality than others. They range from very oily to somewhat dry. Explore the brands available and evaluate their quality for what you choose to make with it. How oily do you need it to be? How has the food been processed? Some are processed with lye. Does that appeal to you? Tahini is light in color. It can create a deliciously creamy substance and has a light, bitter flavor. It works well as a binding agent in hot sauces as well as an oil selection for cold sauces.

Herbs and Spices

I sense hesitancy when it comes to playing with herbs and spices. People seem concerned that there is a "right" use for them and therefore find them threatening. Historically, use of these seasonings was restricted by geography; people ate only what grew locally, occasionally acquiring new items through commerce with traders. Modern transportation and immigration have expanded the possibilities of combinations of herbs and spices. (The latest ethnic taste to come to the United States is Thai food. Its extraordinary use of mint alone promises culinary wonders on the horizon.)

Although the possible combinations are unlimited, there are a few instinctive guidelines that I follow. First, be careful when combining dominant and compatible herbs, and, second, don't use too many. Usually, one to three items is plenty; occasionally I use more if it is clear why each herb or spice has been chosen. Three items make a well-rounded dish, eliminating the chance for confusion and chaos.

Different cultures gather their own special groups of herbs.

HERBS. These give depth and warmth to grain dishes and sauces. These small green plants that radiate vibrations from the ancient civili-

"And scorne not Garlicke like to some that thinke It only makes men wink, and drinke, and stinke"

English proverb

MEDITERRANEAN
Parsley
Oregano
Basil
Rosemary
Fennel
Thyme
Marjoram
Tarragon
Garlic
MIDDLE EAST/
INDIA/NORTH AFRICA
Allspice
Cumin
Coriander
Ginger
Mint
Marjoram
Cinnamon
Turmeric
Saffron
Cilantro
Cardamom
Nutmeg
ORIENT
Ginger
Garlic
Cilantro
Chinese five spice
Mustard
NORTH AMERICA
Sage
Rosemary
Dill

zations of Persia, Egypt, Arabia, Greece, India, and China take us on a culinary journey. Herbs have been used for medicinal, cosmetic, and culinary preparations as well as perfumes and bewitching charms. Fresh herbs are fragrant and radiant. Dried herbs are convenient, but they need to be crushed to release their power. Use two to three times as many fresh herbs as dry because dry herbs are stronger.

Dominant herbs are those with bold, overriding flavors that stand out no matter what you combine them with. Compatible herbs accompany dominant herbs and each other, but most notably blend into a dish gracefully.

SPICES. From the light perfume of saffron to the strong pungency of horseradish, spices add color, flavor, and aroma to grain dishes and sauces. Both dried and fresh spices come from seeds, leaves, bark, and roots. Dry-roasting or sautéing them brings out the aromatic oils in spices, enhancing their strength.

Spices tend to play best with each other when they are of similar dispositions. Sweet, aromatic, and pungent spices can be mixed together, but rely on the sniff-and-taste test.

STORING HERBS AND SPICES. Dry herbs and spices should be stored in dark glass jars, away from heat. This is a good trick if you cook with them a lot, as it is hard to keep them away from the stove. They can keep their potency for about one year. Fresh herbs can be dried by placing them in a paper bag and turning them daily so that they dry out of direct sunlight and the air around them circulates.

Store fresh herbs in the refrigerator. Protect them from drying out by wrapping them in plastic and setting them in a cup of water, like flowers. These will need to be used within one week.

Natural Sweeteners

Grains also provide us with naturally sweet syrups. When sauces and grain dishes call for a sweet taste, barley malt and rice syrup are perfect compatible choices. How can rice be a sweet syrup? If we chew rice for a long time, it mixes with enzymes in our saliva and tastes extremely sweet. Rice syrup is made from rice ground to a meal, cooked in a slurry with water, and stimulated with enzymes until it turns sweet. The slurry is separated from the syrup, leaving a very sticky but relatively whole (complex carbohydrate) sweetener. Barley malt is made similarly, with sprouting and dry-roasting added to the process.

Although these grain-based syrups are quite sweet, they do not alarm blood sugar levels. Blood sugar levels rise and fall in extreme patterns when simple (refined and not complex) sugars are eaten and the missing components of a food (minerals and protein) are drained from the body to make up what was eliminated during processing. Grain sweeteners retain the minerals and protein of the whole grain.

Store grain syrups at room temperature with a tight-fitting lid. When measuring them, oil the cup or spoon first so that these very sticky syrups can leave the measuring utensil without a mess.

DOMINANT HERBS
Cilantro
Tarragon
Marjoram
Sage
Mint

COMPATIBLE HERBS
Basil
Thyme
Chives
Oregano
Dill
Bay leaf
Fennel
Arugula
Lemongrass
Parsley

SWEET SPICES
Allspice
Anise
Cardamom
Cinnamon
Cloves
Nutmeg

AROMATIC SPICES
Coriander seed
Saffron
Fennel seed
Turmeric

PUNGENT/HOT SPICES
Caraway
Cayenne pepper
Cumin
Garlic
Ginger
Horseradish
Mustard
Black and white pepper
Watercress

Part II
Grain Cookery

DEFINITION OF COOKING METHODS FOR GRAIN

FIRST-STAGE COOKING METHODS	DEFINITION	SEASON	ENERGETICS
BAKING	To cook at even, dry heat, especially in an oven	Fall, winter, spring	Steady, even, calm, storing gentle fire
BOILING	To cook in a large volume of rapidly moving liquid	All	Cool, turbulent
PRESSURE-COOKING	To cook in an airtight metal pot that creates steam under pressure	All	Intense strength from gentle, enduring steadfastness
STEEPING	To cook in a measured volume of liquid, first boiling, then over low heat, letting the grain swell into the liquid	All	Balance of hot fire and gentle energy

DEFINITION OF COOKING METHODS FOR GRAIN

SECOND-STAGE COOKING METHODS	DEFINITION	SEASON	ENERGETICS
BRAISING	To steep food in a salty/sour, sometimes sweet, liquid after it is sealed or browned in oil	All	Balance of dynamic and gentle
REFRYING	To heat cooked grain in an oiled skillet	All	Quick, light fire
DEEP-FRY	To submerge in hot oil (375–400°F)	Fall, winter, early spring	Extreme fire energy and subtle turbulence
MARINATING	To soak cooked grain in a cold sauce	Spring, summer, fall	Like resting in a cool, moist place

The more attention we give to preparation, the better the food will taste simply from our efforts. Because whole grains are virginal, quality food, handle them with care. It pays off, as your thoughts, feelings, and actions are transmitted to the people eating the grain. A responsible cook knows this and respects the grain, liquid, and fire that transform a plant into food for humans.

Part II defines and describes the techniques for all stages of cooking and includes recipes that represent each cooking method, at the same time showing the creative process. It is divided into four sections. *Pretreatments* covers the preliminaries of cooking grain, from the necessary washing to various optional methods that affect the texture of the grain before cooking. *First-stage cooking methods* turn raw grains into edible cooked grains and define the energetic quality of the dish. Some first-stage grain dishes are ready to eat as is or with a sauce; others are precursors to additional treatments. *Second-stage cooking methods* transform the flavor and texture of cooked grain with additional cooking and/or seasoning. *Sauces* covers a variety of hot and cold sauces to accompany cooked grain dishes.

Remember, it is almost impossible to ruin grain; too much fire or not enough liquid will scorch it a bit, but even then a mild burnt flavor reminds one of the barbecue; too much liquid, and the grain becomes a soup or sauce. Once you learn the finesse behind these cooking skills, your creativity is limited only by your courage.

Washing Grain

When I was serving as culinary counselor at a large natural foods market, a woman asked me why her brown rice was gray and why there were sticks in it. Apparently she was used to processed grains and it had never occurred to her to wash the whole grain.

Processed grains like instant rice, rolled oats, bulgur, or couscous have been thoroughly washed as part of their processing. In fact, washing them again before cooking will turn them to mush.

Natural whole grains come straight from the fields with minimal handling. Although they have been hulled, cleaned, and separated from miscellaneous organic matter, washing is necessary to remove the dust and fine debris that clings to them, leaving a cleaner, sweeter taste.

There are other reasons to wash the grain besides the dust and debris. The quinoa kernel, for instance, protects itself from solar radiation and insects with a very bitter natural coating called saponin. This coating would ruin the flavor of the cooked grain if not washed off.

Remember to measure your grain *before* you wash it. It is difficult to measure wet grain accurately. Each type of grain responds a little differently to washing. Very small or dry grains (millet, quinoa, buckwheat) with soft outer skins may absorb too much water if they aren't washed quickly.

Washing grain is one of the rare moments we get to touch the grain. It will respond to your feelings and thoughts. Notice how good it feels to have these grains against the palm of your hand, like playing in sand or receiving a special hand massage.

PROCEDURE

- If you are measuring the grain, do so before you wash it, or you will not have an accurate measurement.
- Place measured grain in a large enough bowl to hold at least three times as much cold water as you have grain.
- Massage the grain in the water with the palm of your hand. This will loosen any dust, dirt, and remaining hulls, and bring sticks, dead grains, and rodent droppings to the surface.
- Pour off the top half of the water along with any floating debris. Then pour the rest into a strainer.
- Repeat until you feel the grain is clean and the water is not cloudy, two or three times as necessary.

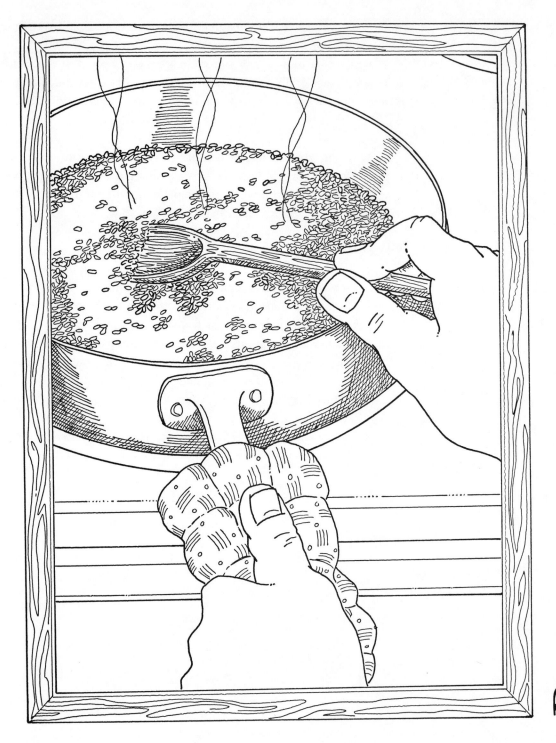

Pretreatments

Dry-roasting, sautéing, and soaking are optional pretreatments that may precede first-stage cooking methods. These treatments exert a fundamental influence on the texture of the finished dish.

Dry-Roasting

Dry-roasting brings out the best in almost any grain. This pretreatment guarantees a nutty aroma and a dry, individual texture. Used with grains that take an exceptionally long time to cook (including bread grains such as barley and whole wheat), this treatment helps the grain open, making it lighter and shortening the cooking time slightly.

To save time, dry-roast several cups of raw grain and store it in an airtight glass jar immediately after it cools. I have kept roasted grain up to a month, ready to use at a moment's notice. Because the grain has been partially cooked, and its energy is out at the surface of the grain, you may choose not to store roasted grain for nutrition's sake. It does lose some power. But I have found that properly sealed grain maintains a strong flavor in the jar, and is pleasant to use even after a month's storage. Use your senses: does it smell dead or alive?

There are two techniques for dry-roasting grain: the oven method and the stove-top method. The greater the quantity you roast, the longer it will take.

THE OVEN METHOD

Use the oven method when roasting more than three cups of grain. This saves time and energy because, although you need to be aware of the roasting grain, you don't have to stand guard as it roasts, and whatever you don't use immediately you can store in glass jars for later use. It is difficult to set a firm amount of time it takes to dry-roast, because the amount of fire used determines how fast it happens. In a moderate oven, a larger quantity of buckwheat can roast as long as 45 minutes, while other grains can be done in 20.

PROCEDURE
- Wash grain and drain in strainer.
- Spread 3 to 6 cups of grain evenly in a 9 × 13-inch baking pan or cookie sheet with sides.
- Place the pan in the middle of a preheated oven. Heat may range from 300 to 375°F, depending on how long you have to tend to the process.
- Stir the grain at 10 to 15 minute intervals until the moisture has evaporated, then stir every 3 to 5 minutes, reaching to the corners, until the grain is done.
- The grain is done when it moves freely, the moisture is completely evaporated, and the aroma and color are magnified.

Store the roasted grain in a glass jar with a tight-fitting lid. Use within a month.

THE STOVE-TOP METHOD

Roasting grain on top of the stove is faster than oven roasting, but requires your full attention. This is a great opportunity to contact the grain, and see, hear, and feel the grains transform. Moving them gently in a repetitive pattern and watching them change to a golden color with a nutty aroma takes on a meditative quality. Be careful, your thoughts and feelings will be received by the grain. Although it is very difficult to ruin a grain dish, I have seen anger and hate help food self-destruct, and an injection of pleasant thoughts bring peace and harmony.

This process can be complete within 15 minutes. When roasting more than one variety of grain at a time, use separate skillets. Each grain will roast in a different length of time.

PROCEDURE

- Measure grain; wash and drain in a strainer.
- Heat a heavy-bottomed skillet over medium-high heat. When the skillet is hot, add the grain.
- Using a bamboo or wooden utensil, move the grain around the skillet in a geometric pattern. (Spirals or zig-zag motions are effective. You may want to do a star design.) Whatever your pattern, make sure each kernel gets turned.
- Once the moisture has evaporated, either reduce the heat to medium or medium-low or begin moving the grains very quickly. One way to do this is by making the grains "leap." Hold the skillet parallel to the stove about seven inches above it or remove it from the stove altogether and hold the skillet at waist level in front of you. With an energetic forward motion, still parallel to the stove or floor, send the skillet away from you for three-quarters of an arm extension. Quickly change the direction, sending the grain into the air as the skillet moves vertically for a moment, and then bring it back to you in the horizontal plane, ready to leap again. A quick jerk sending the grain flying is a thrill. Do this once or twice a minute once the grains are dry and begin to pop.

DRY-ROASTING:
To heat clean grain without oil or liquid until each kernel has a deep color and the aroma of the grain is magnified.

ENERGETICS:
Extra fire for long burning energy.

TEXTURE:
Chewy, individual, fluffy, dry.

FLAVOR:
Nutty.

COMPATIBLE COOKING METHODS:
All first- and second-stage cooking methods are possible, but the texture may be too dry for deep-frying.

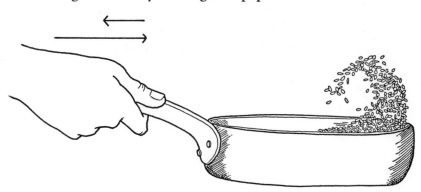

Sautéing

Sautéing is a term borrowed from the French language and cuisine, meaning to cook quickly in a skillet in a small amount of oil. In the French language *sauter* means to leap, and refers to the food "leaping" about in the hot oil. When raw grain is sautéed, each grain is coated with a little bit of oil, putting a seal around its essence. This preliminary treatment creates a texture of individual grains, soft and moist but not sticky. Since oil acts as a bonding agent for seasonings, sautéing vegetables, herbs, and spices along with the grain is a good way to carry their flavors through the dish.

This is not frying or refrying because the grains are raw to begin with. You can use very little oil and lots of vegetables in this method. All grains can be sautéed.

PROCEDURE

- Measure grain; wash and drain.
- Heat a heavy-bottomed skillet and brush it with oil. When the skillet is hot, a small amount of oil will cover the entire pan. If you start with a cold skillet, you will tend to use more oil.
- If using vegetables and herbs, add them now, sealing in their qualities. Then add the grain.
- Move the grain quickly but carefully, as if you were dry-roasting. Maintain a fairly high heat.
- The grain is finished when each one has a light coat of oil.

SAUTÉING:
To seal raw grains in hot oil.
ENERGETICS:
Quick, hot, almost browning; seals in goodness of each grain.
TEXTURE:
Moist, individual grains.
FLAVOR:
Determined by the flavor of oil, herbs, and spices.
COMPATIBLE COOKING METHODS:
Pretreatment – dry-roast; first stage – steep, bake, pressure-cook, boil.

Soaking

Soaking makes grain soft. Soft grain is perfect for young children, infants, the elderly, or people enduring illness. The added liquid in this pretreatment soothes sensitive digestive systems and makes a good texture for breakfast cereals, replacing milled cereals and allowing *whole* grains to be cooked soft. The energy I feel from soaked grains reminds me of the old sayings "drink it in" and "soaking it up." It's a different kind of luscious feeling from that from oil.

The length of soaking time can vary, according to the type of grain and the temperature. Recipes that call for this technique give a range of time, anywhere from two to fourteen hours. The longer you soak grain, the softer the result will be, and long-soaked grain cooks slightly faster. Convenience is probably the biggest factor; soaking grain overnight to cook in the morning or starting it soaking in the morning to cook after work more or less determines the number of hours.

Note that grain soaked for more than fourteen hours at room temperature will ferment and turn sour. (This may be a desirable flavor to create, like that of its relative, sourdough bread.) If you do not want this sour flavor, soak a shorter length of time or keep it cool.

PROCEDURE

- Measure grain and wash it.
- Place it in the pot in which it will be cooked or in a bowl. Cover it with the measured amount of cooking liquid.
- Let it soak for two to fourteen hours.

SOAKING:
To cover raw, roasted, or sautéed grain with a cooking liquid and let it sit for a period of time before the first-stage cooking method.

ENERGETICS:
Slow and careful, as if caring for the ill or injured, elderly, or very young.

TEXTURE:
Wet, heavy, gooey.

FLAVOR:
Bland.

COMPATIBLE COOKING METHODS:
First stage – bake, steep, pressure-cook; second stage – braise.

Cooking Methods

First-Stage

First-stage cooking methods are cooking methods that must be performed before a grain is edible. It is the first time water, fire, and earth (food) are put together. The four basic first-stage methods are baking, boiling, pressure-cooking, and steeping. Steaming, pressure-steaming, and slow cooking in crock pots, etc. are also valid first-stage cooking methods but are not included because they repeat the energetics and textures of these four most common cooking methods. As a general rule, grain prepared in each first-stage method will benefit from a pinch of sea salt.

This chart shows the quantity of liquid needed for each cooking method in the first stage, the general volume of yield, and an estimated time for cooking. The yield for each grain is given, but there is a slight variation in yield between cooking liquids. You will discover these with experience. The first number is the amount of cooking liquid; the second number shows the amount of whole grain. In this case all the ratios are in proportion to one part of grain. The third number gives an estimated duration of cooking time in minutes. Remember, these are ratios, not cup measurements. You may wish to double the volume but don't cut it in half for pressure-cooking, steeping, or baking; less than 1 cup of grain may not cook as well.

Baking

Baking grains allows even expansion as the heat penetrates from all directions simultaneously. The energetic quality of this cooking method feels like a sustained gentle opening of great intensity. It's a gentle gathering and storing of heat. Baked grains have a golden glow around the edges, not unlike a person who has basked in the sun. Baked grains continue to open as long as sufficient liquid is added. This method is very accommodating; by adjusting the temperature of the oven and the amount of cooking liquid, you can control the cooking time to fit your convenience. Too much liquid will create a soft, mushy texture. Measuring the time and liquid will give you some control over the final texture. Preheating the oven is optional, but the times on the grain chart are based on a preheated 350°F oven.

Beyond the delightful texture it gives to the grain, baking is a handy cooking method when you don't have a lot of room left on top of the stove, want to run an errand, or need to heat the house.

FIRST-STAGE COOKING METHODS:
LIQUID, GRAIN, AND TIME

When I first learned to cook whole grains there weren't any recipes, just this kind of chart (and covering only two cooking methods). The first entry under each column is the ratio of cooking liquid to grain; the second, the approximate cooking time in minutes. (Where no figures are given, that particular cooking method and grain are not compatible.) Reduce liquid by ¼ cup if cooking at sea level.

The times given here are just guidelines; how much heat you use, the weight of your cookware, and whether you cook the grain with or without a cover will all require adjustments in the cooking time. Remember, you can't really overcook grain.

GRAIN	BAKE 350°F	BOIL	STEEP	PRESSURE-COOK
RICE				
Short-grain brown	2:1 – 60	8:1 – 27-40	2:1 – 50	1½:1 – 45
Long-grain brown	2:1 – 55	8:1 – 25-35	2:1 – 45	1½:1 – 45
Sweet brown	2:1 – 60	8:1 – 25-30	2:1 – 50	1½:1 – 45
Wild rice	2½:1 – 60	8:1 – 45	2½:1 – 50	1¾:1 – 45
1 cup yields 3 cups				
MILLET				
1 cup yields 3 cups	3½:1 – 45	8:1 – 10	3¼:1 – 40	3:1 – 20
BUCKWHEAT				
1 cup yields 4 cups	2:1 – 20		2:1 – 15	
OATS				
Whole groats	2:1 – 55	8:1 – 20	2:1 –55	1½:1 – 30
1 cup yields 2 cups				
QUINOA				
1 cup yields 4 cups	2:1 – 25	8:1 – 9-12	2:1 – 15	1½:1 – 7
AMARANTH				
1 cup yields 2 cups	2:1 – 35-40	8:1 – 9	2:1 – 30	
TEFF				
1 cup yields 2 cups	3:1 – 30	8:1 – 9	3:1 – 20	
JOB'S TEARS				
1 cup yields 3-4 cups	2½:1 – 90	8:1 – 40	2½:1 – 70	2:1 – 50

PROCEDURE

- Measure and wash grain; pretreat if desired.
- Combine measured cooking liquid, grain, and a pinch of sea salt (if cooking liquid lacks salt) in a baking dish with a cover.
- Place in middle of oven. Bake according to cooking times in grain chart. When grain has swelled, absorbed the liquid, and is open and golden, cooking is complete.
- If desired, baking time may be extended by adding a small amount (⅛ to ¼ cup) additional liquid either before or during cooking. (Longer cooking time may be important if the serving schedule gets delayed, or you want to leave the grain to bake while you focus on something else.)
- Baked grain can stay warm in a turned-off oven, and can be served hot or at room temperature.

BAKING:
To cook in even, dry heat, especially in an oven.
ENERGETICS:
Steady, even, calm; storing gentle fire.
TEXTURE:
Open, slightly sticky, soft.
FLAVOR:
Essence of grain and seasonings, lightly browned.
COMPATIBLE COOKING METHODS:
All.

Baked Quinoa With Squash

1 cup dry-roasted quinoa
2 cups fresh orange juice
1½ teaspoons umeboshi
  paste
½ cup diced onion
1 cup butternut squash,
  cut very small
Parsley for garnish

This delightful and nutritionally complete dish was created during an improvisation class by John Gritton and Tim Triggs. It has no oil, making it a perfect companion for a creamy soup or sauce or a great main course for people who want to avoid fat altogether.

Yield: 4 cups (3–8 servings, depending on how many other dishes are served)

1. Combine ingredients in a 2-quart baking pot and cover.

2. Bake in a preheated 350°F oven for 30 minutes or until grain has absorbed liquid. Mix in parsley before serving.

SERVING SUGGESTIONS: This dish is great all by itself. It could accompany a bean soup and raw vegetable salad. A hot nut sauce, though not necessary, would add elegance.

Process

Pretreatment
DRY-ROAST
First Stage
BAKE
Second Stage
NONE

GRAIN: In order to get a light "pilaf"-style dish, wash the quinoa well, drip-dry a bit, and dry-roast.

COOKING LIQUID: Since I don't allow any preexperienced dishes to be put together during improvisation class, with great courage these gentlemen chose fresh orange juice as the cooking liquid. The sweet orange juice helps balance quinoa's bitter character without making the dish dessert-sweet.

SALT SEASONING: Although umeboshi is usually used in second-stage methods, this improvised dish has no second-stage cooking, so the umeboshi paste replaces sea salt as the salt seasoning in the first stage.

ALTERNATIVE
COOKING METHODS
Pretreatment
NONE
First Stage
STEEP
PRESSURE-COOK

VEGETABLES: Look for a very small butternut squash if possible so you can use the entire vegetable. Judy Jacobsen made this same dish, replacing butternut squash with quartered brussels sprouts.

DECORATIVE VEGETABLE: Parsley makes the orange-toned dish complete.

Job's Tears Baked With Marjoram

This is a very simple but glamourous dish. Job's tears is a distinct grain with each kernel announcing itself as you eat. It's worth waiting through the required long baking time.

Yield: 3½ cups (6–8 servings)

1 cup Job's tears
2½ cups salted bouillon
3 tablespoons fresh marjoram, minced
2 cloves fresh garlic, minced

1. Combine ingredients in a 3-quart baking pot, cover, and bake in a preheated 350°F oven until grain has swelled and absorbed the liquid, about 80 minutes.

SERVING SUGGESTIONS: A sauce will embellish this dish, but it can stand on its own. Using no oil in the grain leaves a lot of options as to the kind of sauce. My first choice would be a vegetable-style sauce, something with decorative vegetables.

Process

GRAIN: Job's tears is the star of this dish, but millet, quinoa, rice, or buckwheat would also be good in this simple combination of ingredients. Check the grain chart on page 74 to see how much cooking liquid is needed. Dry-roasting isn't necessary, but when your dish has only a few ingredients, it enhances the flavor.

COOKING LIQUID: Job's tears love liquid more than other grains. Plain water would keep this pearly white grain almost white in color. If you use water, be sure to use a salt seasoning.

OIL: Most vegetable bouillons suspend flavors in an oil base. If you don't use such a bouillon, add some oil. Any kind will do, except perhaps safflower and canola, which don't carry enough flavor for this dish.

SALT SEASONING: The bouillon was salty in my dish, but if you don't have any bouillon on hand, use sea salt in combination with a salt seasoning like miso, tamari, or umeboshi.

HERBS AND SPICES: Fresh marjoram was most prolific in my garden the day I developed this dish. I could have used tarragon or oregano, or even combined two or three herbs, but because of the simplicity of the dish, a single herb seemed right. A quick, strong addition of garlic satisfied my desire for few ingredients and a flavorful dish.

Pretreatment
NONE
First Stage
BAKE
Second Stage
NONE

ALTERNATIVE
COOKING METHODS
First Stage
STEEP
PRESSURE-COOK

Baked Kasha With Turnips and Mustard Sauce

1 to 3 tablespoons
vegetable oil
1 or 2 cloves garlic,
minced
1 teaspoon dry oregano
1 small onion, diced
1 medium turnip, diced
¼ cup red pepper, diced
1 cup kasha (dry-roasted
buckwheat)
2 cups hot bouillon or
water
½ teaspoon sea salt
(optional)

Make sure you like turnips before you make this dish. They have a lovely but intense bitterness. Kasha is dry-roasted buckwheat.

Yield: 4 servings

1. Choose a baking pot that can be used both on the stove and in the oven. Heat on the stove. Add oil, garlic, oregano, onion, turnip, red pepper, and kasha, sautéing each in order.

2. Combine bouillon with vegetables and kasha. Add sea salt if bouillon is not salted. Cover and bake in preheated 350°F oven about 30 minutes or until the grain has absorbed liquid.

SERVING SUGGESTIONS: I like this served with Cold Mustard Sauce (see p. 178); it adds to the bite of the bitter turnip.

Pretreatment
SAUTÉ
First Stage
BAKE
Second Stage
NONE

Process

This dish was invented at the beginning of cold weather. The contracting feeling from the bitter flavor was quite appealing that day. You can soften the intensity of this dish by eliminating the turnip, or replacing it with cabbage. Mustard sauce accentuates the bitterness slightly, so you might choose a different sauce, such as Mushroom-Onion Sauce (p. 161).

GRAIN: I strongly recommend using dry-roasted rather than raw buckwheat in this dish. You might try the same combination of ingredients, replacing kasha with rice or millet. (See the grain chart on p. 74 for liquid ratios and cooking times.)

OIL: Any mild vegetable oil or ghee will work here. Kasha likes oil; it softens its grainy texture. If using water rather than bouillon, be generous with the oil—2 to 3 tablespoons. (The vegetable bouillon I use has plenty of oil in it, so I use only 1 tablespoon of oil in the recipe.)

SALT SEASONING: If your bouillon is not salted, add ½ teaspoon sea salt or vegetable salt.

COOKING LIQUID: Dilute the bouillon in hot water before adding to grain. The combination of hot liquid and dry-roasted grain gives an especially light, individual texture to the grain.

HERBS AND SPICES: I just happened to pick garlic and oregano for this dish, but others will do as well. Use the sniff-and-taste test. This dish will also be great without any additional herbs or spices. Turnip and buckwheat are both strong enough to carry the dish.

VEGETABLES: The major vegetable is a single turnip, as large or small as you can take, considering the bitter influence. Vegetables of the cabbage family or other root vegetables would be good substitutes for turnips.

ALTERNATIVE
COOKING METHOD
First Stage
STEEP

Baked Lemon-Dill Rice

Twenty years ago, my parents patiently waited for my sister and me to return to eating "normal" foods. While most of our new food introductions passed by them, this dish, served with lemon butter and roasted-tamari almond slivers, made an impression. On occasion they even serve this dish to their dinner guests.

Yield: 3 servings

1 cup brown rice
2 cups water
½ teaspoon sea salt
2 tablespoons dill weed
2 tablespoons minced lemon zest (the colored outer part of the peel)

1. Wash and dry-roast rice by the stove-top method.

2. Combine all ingredients in a heavy, covered baking dish. Bake in a preheated 350°F oven for 50 to 60 minutes, or until grain has swelled and absorbed liquid.

TECHNIQUE NOTE: As long as you have the oven going, you might be tempted to roast the grain in the oven. But with this small quantity, it's really quicker and easier to control on top of the stove.

SERVING SUGGESTIONS: I like this dish served with a dill-flavored nut sauce.

Process

GRAIN: Short-, medium-, and long-grain brown rice, basmati, and specialty rices all work beautifully in this pilaf-style dish.

COOKING LIQUID: To further accentuate the open texture of the rice, bring the water and lemon zest to a boil first, then add the rice and seasonings.

SALT SEASONING: Simply sea salt, to keep the dish white in color.

HERBS AND SPICES: Dill is light in flavor, to match the cooking liquid, so be generous.

Pretreatment
DRY ROAST
First Stage
BAKE
Second Stage
NONE

ALTERNATIVE
COOKING METHODS
First Stage
STEEP
PRESSURE-COOK
BOIL

Baked Oats With Vegetables and Sage

1 tablespoon light sesame
  oil
½ cup diced onion
½ cup diced celery
½ cup diced butternut
  squash
1 cup steel-cut oats
3 tablespoons sage leaves
  (rubbed if dry, minced if
  fresh)
2 tablespoons thyme
1 teaspoon sea salt
2 cups water

GARNISH
Roasted, tamari-flavored
  sunflower seeds

Along with Millet Mash, this dish has a history reaching back to 1968 at the University of Minnesota underground cafeteria, one of the first natural food restaurants in the country. Composed at that time by Leonard Jacobs, this dish was prepared with rolled oats, making it even creamier than this chewy variation. I like the glow around the rim this dish makes as it bakes. For people with wheat sensitivities this dish makes a great substitute for bread stuffing.

Yield: 3 cups (4–6 servings)

1. Heat a heavy-bottomed pot over medium-high heat. Add sesame oil and sauté onions until they are clear. Add celery, squash, herbs, and oats and cook about 5 minutes to seal the edges with oil.

2. Add salt and water. Cover and bake in a preheated 350°F oven for 30 minutes or until grain has absorbed liquid.

SERVING SUGGESTIONS: Tamari-roasted sunflower seeds, cashews, or almonds make a good contrast to the soft texture of baked oats. Because this dish has much flavor to it already, a sauce isn't necessary. If you do want to use a sauce, I suggest something like creamy cauliflower or another combination of vegetables in sauce style #1.

Process

GRAIN: I like the chewiness and energetic quality of steel-cut oats, but whole or rolled oats may also be used for this dish. Allow more cooking time and adjust the amount of cooking liquid when using whole oats (see chart, p. 74).

COOKING LIQUID: I prefer water in this dish because the focus is on what the herbs and vegetables are doing with the grain. If you want to use a different cooking liquid, use vegetable stock.

OIL: Oats need no added fat, but a small amount of oil is needed to enhance the vegetables. Light sesame oil is most compatible with grain and vegetable cookery. Avoid stronger flavored oils, for the same reason as using plain water for the cooking liquid.

SALT SEASONING: Use a simple salt seasoning like sea salt or vegetable salt. Others could be added, but again, the focus is on the vegetables and herbs.

VEGETABLES: Yellow or white onions, celery, and squash all represent different energetic growing styles. Onions hover just below the surface of the earth, giving them a bulbous root energy. Celery reaches high toward the heavens, in a firm, moist stalk, and squash crawls across the surface of the earth as a vine. Their colors offer another kind of harmony: translucent onion, light green celery, and rich orange butternut squash. To make this dish with alternate vegetables, look at color and flavors. Leeks can replace or join the onion; asparagus, another upright stalk, could join or replace celery; and carrot could replace the squash, maintaining the orange color and balancing the leek energy with its root quality.

HERBS AND SPICES: Don't be alarmed by the great quantity of strong herbs in this dish. Oats are notorious for being able to soak up flavor. Even sage, a dominant herb, disappears in the density of oats. Thyme and sage work well together, as we all know from turkey stuffing. If you change the herbs in this dish, use at least one dominant herb, such as cilantro, tarragon, or rosemary.

Pretreatment
NONE
First Stage
BAKE
Second Stage
NONE

ALTERNATIVE
COOKING METHODS
Pretreatment
DRY-ROAST
First Stage
STEEP
PRESSURE-COOK

Baked Brown Rice
With Basil and Onions

2 cups brown rice
4 cups water
½ cup sliced yellow onion
3 tablespoons fresh basil
½ teaspoon sea salt

Notice how similar this dish is to Job's Tears Baked With Marjoram (p. 77); different grain and different herbs, but the same cooking method. Since this grain has not been dry-roasted, choose a temperature for the cooking liquid to get the texture you want: hot liquid makes a chewier, dry, individual character; cold yields a heavier, softer, moister dish.

Yield: 3 cups (4 servings)

1. Wash and drain rice.

2. Combine rice, water, onions, basil, and sea salt in a covered baking dish. Bake in a preheated 350°F oven for 50 to 60 minutes.

SERVING SUGGESTIONS: Without oil in the grain dish, a sauce is in order. Bean, vegetable, nut, and clear sauces are all appropriate with this versatile baked dish.

Process

Pretreatment
NONE
First Stage
BAKE
Second Stage
NONE

GRAIN: This could be any grain. Check the grain chart on page 74 for measurement of liquid and time.

COOKING LIQUID: Flavored water will help this simple dish. A vegetable stock, a little wine, a bay leaf, and tomato juice are all options for changing this dish.

OIL: No oil makes a good opportunity for a nut sauce or vegetable sauce style #2.

SALT: Some form of salt is needed for transforming the cellular structure of the grain in a first-stage method. Umeboshi could also work.

HERBS AND SPICES: Anything goes here. Have fun! Try to keep herbs and spices compatible. For example, if you choose fragrant herbs, stay with herbs; if you choose sweet spices such as nutmeg, cinnamon, cloves, etc., stay with those (although basil and cinnamon may be good together). Use the sniff-and-taste test when in doubt.

VEGETABLES: Yellow or purple onions, leeks, shallots, and garlic are all interchangeable. I prefer to keep this dish simple, so I have not used any other vegetables. If you want to add other decorative vegetables such as sweet red peppers, sauté them and the onions first so they keep their individuality.

ALTERNATIVE
COOKING METHOD
NONE

Baked Long-Grain Rice in Juice With Pine Nuts

I was inventing dishes with juice as cooking liquid when this one came about. What a surprise! I thought it would be too sweet to serve as a main dish, but the elegance and well-rounded aromatic flavors are irresistible and not too sweet.

Yield: 4 servings

1. Wash and dry-roast rice in a skillet on top of the stove.

2. Combine all ingredients in a heavy covered baking dish. Bake in a preheated 350°F oven for 50 to 60 minutes, or until grain has absorbed liquid.

3. Dry-roast pine nuts in a skillet on top of the stove. Sprinkle with tamari and toss until dry. Mix into cooked rice right before serving.

TECHNIQUE NOTE: To make ginger juice, grate fresh ginger onto a plate with a fine box grater or a special ginger grater; squeeze the shreds with your fingertips to extract the juice.

SERVING SUGGESTIONS: Serve hot. A sauce is not necessary for such a tasty dish, but you could use a clear or vegetable-style sauce to embellish the meal.

1 cup long-grain brown rice
1 cup pineapple-orange juice
1 cup water
½ teaspoon sea salt
1 teaspoon ginger juice
1-inch piece cinnamon stick

GARNISH
½ cup pine nuts
1 tablespoon tamari

Process

GRAIN: The character of long-grain rice suits this pilaf-style dish as it easily opens to receive flavors from the cooking liquid and spices. It makes a great background for the exotic flavors of these spices and cooking liquids.

OIL: Oil is not required for this cooking method. Pine nuts supply a little oil.

HERBS AND SPICES: Cinnamon stick is easily removed and gives a delicate, distinct flavor. Other sweet spices such as cloves, cardamom, or nutmeg could be added.

VEGETABLES: There aren't any vegetables in this fruity composition. You could use parsley as a decorative vegetable.

Pretreatment
NONE
First Stage
BAKE
Second Stage
NONE

ALTERNATIVE
COOKING METHODS
First Stage
STEEP
PRESSURE-COOK

Buckwheat and Greens
in Filo Pastry

3 or 4 large leaves kale
1 clove garlic, minced
2 tablespoons fresh basil
  or 1 tablespoon dried
1½ tablespoons apple
  cider vinegar
2 teaspoons olive oil
¼ teaspoon sea salt
6 whole artichoke hearts
  (canned or marinated),
  quartered
4 red radishes, sliced very
  thin
12 Calamata (black Greek)
  olives (optional)
8 sheets filo pastry
6 tablespoons ghee, or
  more as needed
1 cup kasha, cooked in
  bouillon

This dish shows how leftovers can be transformed into a whole new dish. I wanted to make something like kasha knishes, but each attempt was vetoed as too heavy. So I changed the pastry from puff pastry to filo and added some of a marinated kale salad that had been sitting around the refrigerator for a few days. The results were light, tangy, crispy pouches suitable for appetizers or traveling food. This is a rare example of baking as a second-stage cooking method.

Yield: 8 pouches

1. Cook kale in a covered saucepan with just enough lightly salted water to cover the bottom of the pot. When the stems are evenly light green and the leaves are brilliant green, plunge them into cold water. Squeeze, unroll, and stack the leaves and cut them into small pieces.

2. Mix garlic, vinegar, sea salt, olive oil, and basil together in a large bowl. Add the cooked kale, radish, artichoke hearts, and pitted olives and toss to coat with dressing.

3. Melt ghee in a small heavy saucepan. Take out one sheet of filo at a time, keeping the rest covered with a damp towel. Brush entire sheet with ghee and fold a third of the long side over the middle. Brush the new top surface with ghee and fold the other side over it, forming a thin rectangle the length of the original sheet. Brush the top with ghee and place 2 to 3 tablespoons each of the cooked kasha and kale salad near one end. Fold one corner over the stuffing, making a triangular end, then roll up the triangle in the rest of the sheet as if folding a flag (remember this from your scouting days?). Repeat with remaining filo and filling.

4. Bake packets on an ungreased sheet pan in a 350°F oven for 10 minutes or until crisp and golden brown.

SERVING SUGGESTIONS: These pouches make a good accompaniment to soup, but I also serve them with the cauliflower sauce on page 163. This sauce has relatively little oil, so it complemented the buttery filo. Or serve with Mock Mustard Sauce (p. 160) as appetizers.

Process

GRAIN: I made this with roasted buckwheat that had first been baked in bouillon with green onions and no added oil. These pouches could also be made with cooked millet, rice, quinoa, or Job's tears.

COOKING LIQUID: The vinegar in the kale salad dressing (the same as the basic herbal marinade on p. 173) "cuts through" and lightens this notoriously heavy-tasting grain.

OIL: This grain loves oil, especially when cooked with very little in the first stage. The ghee in the pastry generously supplies it.

SALT SEASONING: A small amount of sea salt in the marinade is all that is needed here. Play with other salt seasonings in the marinade.

VEGETABLES: Collard or mustard greens or regular or exotic cabbages could substitute for the kale.

Pretreatment
DRY-ROAST
First Stage
STEEP
Second Stage
BAKE

ALTERNATIVE
COOKING METHODS
NONE

Millet With Tarragon
Baked in Nut Milk and Wine

1 cup millet, washed and
   drained
3½ cups cashew milk
   (blend ⅓ cup raw
   cashews with 3½ cups
   water)
1 teaspoon vegetable salt
1 tablespoon dried
   tarragon
⅓ cup dry white wine

This dish was my first attempt to use nut milk as a cooking liquid. I was shocked at how rich and luscious it was. In fact, it felt a little heavy until rescued by the wine. This baking method is easy. The most important thing to remember about baking is to have a tight-fitting cover. To check to see if the dish is done, insert a knife or fork vertically to the bottom and spread the grains apart just enough to see if any liquid remains. Don't stir the grain until it is done.

Yield: 4 servings

1. Combine all ingredients except wine in a heavy 2-quart baking pot. Cover and bake in a preheated 350°F oven for 45 minutes. Remove from oven, mix in wine, cover, and let sit for 5 minutes.

SERVING SUGGESTIONS: I recommend a vegetable sauce and a crisp salad with no oil in the dressing.

Process

Pretreatment
NONE
First Stage
BAKE
Second Stage
NONE

ALTERNATIVE
COOKING METHODS
Pretreatment
DRY-ROAST
First Stage
STEEP
PRESSURE-COOK

GRAIN: Try this dish with other grains such as quinoa, Job's tears, or rice. Check the grain chart on page 74 for time and the amount of cooking liquid.
COOKING LIQUID: Nut milk makes this a rich and sensual dish. Add ⅓ cup more water during baking if you don't use wine.
SALT SEASONING: Vegetable salt can be replaced with sea salt or 2 teaspoons umeboshi paste.
HERBS AND SPICES: Tarragon is my favorite herb for this dish, but dill, oregano, marjoram, arugula, cinnamon, and nutmeg all make baked millet delicious. Be sure to release the flavors of the herbs by rubbing them between your thumb and fingers. Season to your taste, remembering that nut milk absorbs more strength of flavor than you initially think.
VEGETABLES: Decorative vegetables are not included in this recipe, but red pepper, green peas, or parsley would make a lovely presentation.

Boiling

Boiling is the most misused term in grain cookery. If I asked you how to prepare rice or oats or millet, you would probably say, "Boil them." But what most people describe as boiling is really steeping (see p. 95).

True boiling (cooking in a large volume of boiling liquid, as in cooking pasta) can be a refreshing alternative to other first-stage cooking methods. The ratio should be around eight parts liquid to one part grain. In the boiling pot, grains cook freely, the surface of each grain having contact with the liquid, so they maintain an individual, somewhat chewy character. More than the heat (as boiling, at 212°F, does not store much heat), the turbulent action of the liquid cooks the grain.

Unlike the other first-stage cooking methods, it isn't necessary to measure precise amounts of grain and cooking liquid. The leftover boiling liquid can be used as stock or in soups and sauces.

Energetically, boiling has been associated with anger, but I have also experienced a feeling of turbulence over the joy in love and at the source of a creative idea. This is a delightful cooking method all year round, and especially good for soaking up cold sauces. I like to flavor the boiling bath with fresh ginger slices, lemon zest, or garlic.

The times for boiling grain on the grain chart are based on my home altitude of around 5,000 feet. Allow less time for lower altitudes and more for higher. Most important, watch the grain, not the clock.

BOILING:
To cook in a large volume (8:1) of rapidly moving liquid (212°F or 100°C) in an open pot.
ENERGETICS:
Cool, turbulent.
TEXTURE:
Saturated, individual, chewy (al dente), uneven.
FLAVOR:
Plain.
COMPATIBLE COOKING METHODS:
Pretreatment – dry-roast; second stage – marinate, refry, braise.

PROCEDURE

- Wash grain and pretreat if desired.
- Bring liquid to a rapid boil. Add ¼ teaspoon sea salt per quart of liquid.
- Add grain and adjust heat to maintain a rapid boil. Do not cover.
- The grain chart on page 74 will serve as a guide for timing, but use your instincts, sight, touch, and taste to determine if the grain is done. It is easy to overcook grain in this method. Slightly overcooked grains do firm up a bit as they cool.
- Pour cooked grain and liquid through a fine mesh strainer, allowing the excess liquid to drip through. To cool grain for a second-stage dish, drop it into a cold water bath and drain it again to stop the cooking and preserve the texture. To keep grain warm, place the strainer back over the hot liquid and cover. If you will be keeping it warm, undercook it a bit so that as it stands it will not get too mushy. Shake the strainer occasionally.

Oat Groat Soup With Mustard and Thyme

1 cup whole oat groats
2 tablespoons light
    sesame oil
3 tablespoons minced
    garlic (3 cloves)
½ cup diced onion
½ cup diced carrots
1 cup diced celery
⅛ cup diced sweet red
    pepper
½ cup chopped parsley
2 tablespoons thyme
    leaves
3 tablespoons oregano
    leaves
7 cups water
2 inches kombu sea
    vegetable
2½ teaspoons vegetable salt
1 bay leaf
4 heaping teaspoons
    prepared mustard
Pepper to taste

Pretreatment
DRY-ROAST
First Stage
BOIL
Second Stage
NONE

This dish is the product of fixing a mistake. I had accidentally used much too much cooking liquid in a baked oat dish. I could have persisted in baking the soupy mixture, but instead I accepted the challenge of turning it into a good soup.

Yield: 6 servings

1. Wash and dry-roast oats.

2. Heat a heavy-bottomed soup pot over medium-high heat and add oil. Sauté garlic, herbs, vegetables, and grain, sealing them one at a time.

3. Add water, kombu, vegetable salt, and bay leaf. Bring to a slow boil and simmer for 45 minutes. Add mustard and pepper during the last 15 minutes of cooking.

SERVING SUGGESTIONS: This dish is best served with other dishes like a tempeh burger, or a salad and a vegetable protein dish.

Process

GRAIN: Oats present a pleasant chewy eating experience, even in soup. If you use a different grain, adjust the cooking time according to its character (see the grain chart on p. 74).

COOKING LIQUID: Water, sautéed vegetables, herbs, spices, and kombu create a good broth. Kombu extracts the best flavor the vegetables and grain have to offer. Oats emit warmth into the broth, and the herbs and spices round out the depth of flavors.

OIL: Because of the multiple flavors in this broth, I like the not-too-aggressive flavor of light sesame oil. Ghee would be a good alternative.

SALT SEASONING: Vegetable salt contributes to the flavor of the broth in two ways: like other forms of salt, it helps release the flavors of the vegetables, herbs, and grain; and it brings with it additional vegetable flavors.

HERBS AND SPICES: Oats absorb more flavor than other grains, so they need strong herbs and spices such as thyme, oregano, mustard, garlic, and bay leaf. If making this dish with other grains, rice for instance, you might want to cut back on the amount of these ingredients.

ALTERNATIVE
COOKING METHODS
NONE

Quinoa and Herb Broth

This dish was spontaneously created during a ritual welcoming a new teacher into the school. Each item was specifically chosen to symbolize nature's elements – earth, air, fire, water, and metal. In their simplicity, the ingredients and cooking method represent the essence and art of cooking. During the ritual, I didn't stir the food with a utensil, only gently tossing the pan once or twice during the sauté step.

Yield: 4 servings

1. Heat a heavy pot over medium-high heat and add oil. Sauté green onion, arugula, and quinoa in oil, sealing one at a time.
2. Add water and salt. Bring to a slow boil and cook uncovered for 7 to 9 minutes or until the spirals from quinoa are visible. Add red pepper and cook 1 minute before serving.

1 teaspoon dark sesame oil
1 green onion, roots and all, thinly sliced
6 leaves fresh arugula, minced
¼ cup quinoa, washed
4 cups water
1 teaspoon sea salt
Slivers of red pepper for garnish

Process

GRAIN: I prefer the grain al dente, when the individual grains are still a bit chewy in this dish. If you prefer them softer, cook a few minutes more. Other grains that would be good are millet, rice, amaranth, and teff.

COOKING LIQUID: I kept the cooking liquid simple for the ritual, but vegetable stock would be a great alternative. Water in a dish with few ingredients gives a very clear and clean feeling to the broth.

OIL: Dark sesame oil was chosen for its strong flavor. Olive oil would be a good alternative. Another option is no oil.

SALT SEASONING: Pure sea salt gives the broth a clear color and accentuates the individual ingredients as they come together. You could use umeboshi vinegar, tamari, or miso, but bear in mind that they will change the appearance of the broth.

HERBS AND SPICES: Arugula, a fresh culinary herb most frequently served raw as an addition to salad, has the dual quality of being able to blend into a dish as well as stand alone with its well-rounded flavor.

VEGETABLES: Green onion alone rounds out the flavors of this dish. I use the entire vegetable—tendril root to tubular green. When a dish has few ingredients, I almost always use a food from the onion family; other possibilities are leek, purple onion, and shallots.

Pretreatment
NONE
First Stage
BOIL
Second Stage
NONE

ALTERNATIVE
COOKING METHODS
NONE

Tomato Soup With Wehani Rice

2 tablespoons olive oil
1 large onion and/or leek, diced
4 cloves garlic
3 tablespoons dried marjoram leaves, or 6 tablespoons fresh
4 tablespoons dried basil leaves, or 8 tablespoons fresh
4 tablespoons dried oregano leaves, or 8 tablespoons fresh
1 tablespoon fennel seed, crushed or ground a bit
1 cup wehani rice
1 (28 oz.) can tomato purée
8 cups water or bouillon
1 or 2 bay leaves
2 teaspoons vegetable salt (omit if using salted bouillon)
2 cups cashew milk (optional – see Cooking Liquid)
Pepper to taste
Tamari to taste

Pretreatment
SAUTÉ
First Stage
BOIL
Second Stage
NONE

ALTERNATIVE
COOKING METHODS
NONE

This dish feels like a cross between creamy tomato soup and Spanish rice. In the beginning it is soup, but as it sits it becomes a soft rice dish. The most difficult part of this dish is getting the flavors strong enough. If this recipe is too wimpy for you, I suggest using full-strength bouillon or vegetable stock and twice as many herbs as you think you will need.

Yield: 10–12 servings

1. Heat a heavy-bottomed soup pot over medium-high heat and add oil. Sauté vegetables, herbs, and rice in oil, sealing them one at a time.

2. Add tomato purée, water, or bouillon, bay leaf, and vegetable salt. Bring to a slow boil and cook for 60 minutes, or until grains have opened.

3. Add cashew milk and pepper to taste. Simmer for 10 minutes or more. Adjust seasoning with tamari to taste.

Process

GRAIN: Wehani rice gives a nutty flavor to this all-American dish, but any style of rice will work. If you want the dish to remain a soup, decrease the amount of rice.

COOKING LIQUID: Altogether, you need at least 10 cups cooking liquid to make this a soup. Using up to a quarter nut milk makes an especially creamy, substantial soup, but this is totally optional. If not using nut milk, add 2 cups water or vegetable stock.

OIL: Olive oil is my first choice for this dish because of its herbal nature, but any vegetable oil or ghee works well in this style of dish.

SALT SEASONING: Vegetable salt is a good place to begin, but you might need more seasoning for the final touch. A light miso may work, but could interfere with the color, so it's probably best to stick with vegetable or sea salt. Be sure to cook it into the dish.

HERBS AND SPICES: I like to indulge in the flavors of garlic, oregano, basil, marjoram, and fennel. Make sure you crush dry herbs first to release their potency. I put fennel seeds in my pepper mill, with or without pepper.

Millet-Miso Vegetable Stew

Whether you choose all root vegetables or a combination of stalk, vine, and roots, this hearty stew is sweet and nourishing. Always include some kind of onion.

Yield: 4–6 servings

1. Heat a heavy-bottomed soup pot over medium-high heat and add oil. Sauté vegetables, sealing them one at a time. Add kombu stock and bring to a slow boil.

2. Add millet and sea salt and simmer for 30 minutes. Season with miso, tamari, and wine before serving.

SERVING SUGGESTIONS: Balance the meal with salad and a source of protein.

2 teaspoons toasted
 sesame oil
½ cup coarsely cut onion
1 cup coarsely cut carrot
½ cup coarsely cut
 parsnip
½ cup coarsely cut celery
¼ cup coarsely cut sweet
 red pepper
6 cups kombu stock
½ cup millet, dry-roasted
½ teaspoon sea salt
2 tablespoons barley miso
2 tablespoons tamari
2 tablespoons wine
 (optional)

Process

GRAIN: Millet has a great way of expanding into stew. Quinoa, Job's tears, and teff are good alternatives. Dry-roasting enhances the flavor. Sautéing the roasted grain is optional, but helps the grain keep its shape.

COOKING LIQUID: Kombu stock or another vegetable broth will give more flavor to this dish than water. A favorite variation is to use the surplus broth from cooking garbanzo beans. Add the beans to the stew too.

SALT SEASONING: Sea salt helps vegetables release their flavors into the broth. Miso gives a mellow, winy flavor to the broth, and a bit of tamari before serving fine-tunes the flavor.

HERBS AND SPICES: This dish can stand on the flavors of the vegetables, grain, salt seasoning, oil, and cooking liquid, with no herbs or spices added. If you like, try shallot, bay leaf, and fresh ground pepper.

VEGETABLES: The major vegetables should be cut in sizable pieces as befits a stew. Even red pepper could be a major vegetable in this dish. I also like burdock, cauliflower, and leek in addition to or in place of the vegetables listed.

Pretreatment
DRY-ROAST
SAUTÉ
First Stage
BOIL
Second Stage
NONE

ALTERNATIVE
COOKING METHOD
Pretreatment
SAUTÉ
First Stage
NONE

Wild Rice Soup

1 tablespoon vegetable oil
  or ghee
1 or 2 shallots or large
  cloves of garlic, minced
1 small onion, diced
2 ribs celery, diced
1 tablespoon dried sage,
  or to taste
1 tablespoon dried thyme,
  or to taste
¾ cup wild rice, washed
  and drained
7 cups water or bouillon
1 teaspoon vegetable salt
  (reduce or omit if using
  salted bouillon)
Tamari or shoyu to taste

When boiled together, wild rice, vegetables, and herbs bleed their flavors into a delicious broth, and the chewy texture of the rice complements the soft vegetables. I made this soup on the first snowy day of fall. I had only onion and celery at hand and I knew it needed a strong character in the leading role, so I chose wild rice.

Yield: 4–6 servings

1. Heat a heavy-bottomed soup pot over medium-high heat and add oil. Sauté vegetables, herbs, and wild rice in oil, sealing each one at a time.

2. Add water or bouillon and vegetable salt. Bring to a slow boil and cook for 60 minutes, or until grains have opened. Adjust seasoning with tamari to taste.

TECHNIQUE NOTE: The longer this sautéing process, the stronger the flavor of the soup. By sautéing in the soup pot, you collect a residue of flavors that might be lost if you transfer from a skillet. If you must use a skillet to sauté the vegetables, herbs, and grain, save the collection of browned goodness at the bottom of the skillet by running about ¼ cup of the cooking liquid into the skillet, loosening it with a spoon and pouring this into the soup pot.

SERVING SUGGESTIONS: This soup makes a great first course for a vegetable dinner with winter squash, a green vegetable, and salad, with some vegetable protein in one of the dishes. If you include the other hearty vegetables in this soup, it becomes the main attraction. Bread and green salad with marinated beans would be good company.

Process

GRAIN: This dish is a great way to show off the flavors of wild rice. Because of the sparse number of ingredients in this soup, an alternative grain should have a strong character; try Job's tears or wehani rice.

OIL: The oil plays a secondary role in flavor but a primary role in function. Olive, corn, or light sesame oil or ghee will work equally well. I avoid dark sesame oil because its strong flavor is not compatible with the strong flavor of wild rice. (When using a grain with milder flavor, for example brown rice, dark sesame oil is the perfect choice.) The main purpose of the oil here is to seal the grain and the cut vegetables so the essence of each is not totally destroyed in the simmering bath. Oil also helps the flavor of the herbs and spices blend throughout the liquid and the grain.

SALT SEASONINGS: Which salt or salt seasonings to use depends on the broth. If using salted bouillon or salted stock, you won't need any salt to help cook the grain and vegetables. Depending on how salty the stock is, you may or may not need to add a salt seasoning like tamari or miso at the end. If it is too salty, use white wine or mirin to balance the taste.

COOKING LIQUID: Chicken stock is perfect, if you use it. Water is too neutral, because there are only two vegetables, and not a lot of them at that. So, to boost the strength of the broth and keep a large ratio of vegetables and grain to liquid, I use a homemade vegetable stock or bouillon cubes. When using salted bouillon cubes I dilute them more than usual so that there is room for my choice of salt seasoning at the end.

HERBS AND SPICES: Sage, thyme, and garlic all support the earthy flavor of wild rice—just think of a Thanksgiving dinner. Each of these flavors is dominant in character and strength yet they are quite compatible, and a great help to a broth that is mostly water.

VEGETABLES: Cut the vegetables into pieces that will fit in a spoon but are not so small that they get lost. Using only onions and celery keeps this dish very simple. Other vegetables that would change the character but embellish the flavor of this soup are mushrooms, parsnips, peppers, and squash.

Pretreatment
SAUTÉ
First Stage
BOIL
Second Stage
NONE

ALTERNATIVE
COOKING METHODS
Pretreatment
DRY-ROAST
First Stage
PRESSURE-COOK

Hot and Sour Rice Soup

7 cups water
3-inch piece kombu sea
  vegetable
1 cup long-grain brown
  rice, dry-roasted
2 teaspoons sea salt
2 tablespoons raw cashew
  butter
3 tablespoons fresh basil
  leaves
3 tablespoons ginger juice
3 tablespoons fresh lemon
  juice
¼ teaspoon cayenne
  pepper
Umeboshi vinegar, miso,
  or tamari to taste

Unlike other boiled grain dishes, this soup cooks slowly, and the cooking liquid is savored, not discarded. The flavors remind me of the Greek lemon and egg soup, *avgolemono*.

Yield: 6–8 servings

1. Bring water and kombu to a slow boil. Add rice and sea salt and simmer for 30 minutes.

2. Remove kombu and add remaining ingredients. Simmer until flavors integrate, about 10 minutes.

3. Adjust taste with umeboshi vinegar.

SERVING SUGGESTIONS: Serve warm with bean pâté, bread, and a vegetable side dish.

Process

Pretreatment
DRY-ROAST
First Stage
BOIL
Second Stage
NONE

GRAIN: Long-grain brown rice is best for its quality of openness and the way it survives the boiling method, especially when dry-roasted before being put in the broth. Millet, Job's tears, quinoa, and teff are other possibilities.
COOKING LIQUID: Kombu stock creates substance; ginger and lemon juice are accent liquids.
OIL: Cashew butter gives the broth a creamy hint of nut milk.
SALT SEASONING: Sea salt provides the basic salt seasoning. If the soup needs a sour flavor in the final seasoning, use umeboshi; otherwise, use miso or tamari.
HERBS AND SPICES: When I developed this dish, I thought basil, cayenne, and ginger made an interesting new combination. Then I found out they are often combined in Thai and other Southeast Asian cuisines.
VEGETABLES: Kombu is the only vegetable element, and it is removed before serving. I like having a soup that is just grain and broth; it's different.

ALTERNATIVE
COOKING METHODS
Pretreatment
SOAK

Steeping

Steeping is the best known method for cooking grain. The grain and liquid are brought to a boil, then cooked over low heat until the grain is done and the liquid absorbed. This is the only method most people know. The energetics we receive from steeped grain is the balance of two extremes—"bring to a boil and reduce to a simmer," sound familiar?

Steeped grain is perfect for all second-stage cooking methods.

PROCEDURE

- Measure, wash, and drain grain.
- Measure cooking liquid (see grain chart, p. 74). Combine grain and liquid in a pot with a cover. Add a pinch of sea salt if cooking liquid is unsalted.
- Bring to a rapid boil; reduce heat to medium-low. Use a flame tamer after 30 minutes.
- For variation in texture, boil the liquid first, then add the grain. This gives the grain a more open and individual texture, and also gives you a chance to flavor or color the cooking liquid.
- Do not stir the grain while it is cooking. The steam tunnels created during the cooking process become channels for distributing heat evenly. If these are broken, some grains could be raw, while others are cooked.
- The grain is done when all the liquid has been absorbed into the grain, and the grains are cooked through the center. Check this by inserting a utensil vertically to the bottom of the pot and moving it gently sideways to look for liquid.
- (Optional.) Place a clean cloth over the grain as it sits in the pot to absorb the extra moisture. This is especially good to do if you desire an individual texture.

STEEPING:
To cook a measured amount of grain in a measured amount of liquid in a covered pot until the grain has swelled, absorbing all the liquid.

ENERGETICS:
Balance of hot fiery energy and gentleness.

TEXTURE:
Unless modified by pre-treatments, grain is balanced—not too dry, not too wet, not too individual, not too sticky, not too interesting.

FLAVOR:
Plain.

COMPATIBLE COOKING METHODS:
All.

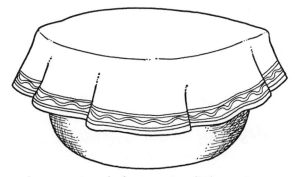

An extra touch for creating light grain.

Mr. Sanford's Breakfast Oats

1 cup steel-cut oats,
  rinsed
1½ cups apple juice
1½ cups water
¼ teaspoon sea salt
¼ cup raisins
½ teaspoon ground
  cinnamon or a 2-inch
  piece cinnamon stick
¼ cup pecan pieces
  (optional)

Mr. Sanford was a dear man and an excellent cook, who, at the time I met him, was successfully staving off cancer and old age with wit and diet. As a guest in his home I was treated to this convalescent breakfast each day. He prepared it overnight in a crock pot. The selection of dry fruit would vary, and some days he would slip in an extra touch of sweetener like molasses or barley malt. This recipe is not as sweet as his.

Yield: 3 cups (4 servings)

1. Soak oats in apple juice and water 2 to 6 hours or overnight in a heavy pot.

2. Combine oats, juice, water, raisins, cinnamon, and salt. Cover and bring to a gentle boil. Reduce heat to medium-low. Steep until all the liquid is absorbed, 30 to 60 minutes. Use a flame tamer to moderate heat.

3. Mix pecans in just before serving. Remove cinnamon stick (if used) before serving.

SERVING SUGGESTIONS: If this dish isn't too sweet it makes a good breakfast. Mr. Sanford indulged by smothering his serving with almond amasake, a kind of rice milk prepared from sweet and fermented rice and water (look for it in health food markets). I like it best with apple juice as the major cooking liquid and served as a dessertlike pudding.

Process

Pretreatment
SOAK
First Stage
STEEP
Second Stage
NONE

ALTERNATIVE
COOKING METHODS
Pretreatment
DRY-ROAST
First Stage
BAKE

GRAIN: Rolled oats make a better substitute than whole oats. We are going for a creamy texture.
COOKING LIQUID: Up to half apple juice adds just the right touch of sweetness. If you want a sweeter dish, use all apple juice, although to my taste this turns the dish into a dessert.
SALT SEASONING: Simple sea salt allows the flavors to blend without intruding.
FRUIT: Raisins add sweetness. Other fresh or dried fruit like apricots or peaches are good substitutes. Don't use too many.
HERBS AND SPICES: Other sweet spices are optional: cardamom, cloves, nutmeg, etc.

Oats, Onions, and Thyme

Dishes don't come much easier than this one. It was inspired on a day when there wasn't any time to cook, and there wasn't any food in the house save an onion and some grain. I chose oats because they cook quickly. To save a little more time, I used the teapot to heat water while sautéing the vegetables and grain.

Yield: 3 cups (3–4 servings)

2 cups boiling water
½ tablespoon dark sesame oil
1½ cups very thinly sliced onion
1 tablespoon thyme
1 cup steel-cut oats
½ teaspoon sea salt

1. Heat pot over medium-high heat and add oil. Sauté onions and thyme, sealing them before adding the oats. If you have time, the longer you sauté the onions the sweeter the dish. Don't hesitate to almost burn them, but do it slowly. When onions are brown, add oats and sauté them for about 2 minutes.

2. Combine boiling water with oats, onions, and thyme. Cover and reduce heat to medium-low. Steep until all the liquid is absorbed, about 30 minutes. Use a flame tamer to moderate heat.

SERVING SUGGESTIONS: Marinated bean salad or a vegetable and bean soup would be a perfect accompaniment to this main dish.

Process

GRAIN: Any style of oat (whole, steel cut, or rolled) works beautifully in this dish. Try buckwheat, millet, or quinoa in the same process, checking the grain chart on page 74 for variables in liquid and time.
COOKING LIQUID: Water keeps this dish simple and allows the thyme and onions to show their strength.
OIL: Because there are so few ingredients, this dish needs a rich-flavored oil to contribute a strong flavor. Olive oil is also a possibility.
SALT SEASONING: Sea salt is the most efficient salt seasoning for bringing out the best flavors of these simple ingredients.
HERBS AND SPICES: Because of the simplicity of the dish, only one herb was chosen, but a bouquet of flavors could also work, perhaps marjoram, basil, and bay leaf. But keep it simple. If one ingredient works, why add others?
VEGETABLES: Ah, onions! What more can I say? Such a pure fruit of the earth with a spirit of fire. All alone, onions elevate this humble grain into magnificence. Slice them very thin so they almost melt into the dish.

Pretreatment
NONE
First Stage
STEEP
Second Stage
NONE

ALTERNATIVE
COOKING METHODS
Pretreatment
DRY-ROAST
First Stage
BAKE
PRESSURE-COOK

Sweet Almond Rice Pudding

1 cup raw brown rice
Water to cover rice
½ cup almonds
3 cups water
¼ cup maple syrup
1½-inch piece cinnamon
    stick
1 teaspoon vanilla
Pinch of sea salt

Rice pudding is a traditional dish, usually loaded with rich butter, milk, eggs, and sugar. Whether you use this dish as an in-between meal treat or a hearty dessert, the wholeness of this pudding is rich, sweet, and filling. This dish was created to be an example of nut milk used as a cooking liquid. Originally it was prepared with basil to be served as a main course, but there were overwhelming messages to use sweet spices instead.

Yield: 3 cups (4–6 servings)

1. Wash rice and soak in water to cover for 4 to 12 hours. Strain after kernels have softened (see Soaking, p. 71, for more on this technique). Strain rice. You may wish to save the soaking water as stock.

2. Blend almonds in 3 cups water and strain through cheesecloth into pot.

3. Combine rice, nut milk, maple syrup, cinnamon stick, vanilla, and sea salt in a heavy pot. Cover, bring to a slow boil, and reduce heat to medium-low. Steep until all the liquid is absorbed, about 60 minutes. Use a flame tamer to moderate heat.

Process

Pretreatment
SOAK
First Stage
STEEP
Second Stage
NONE

GRAIN: With the assistance of a good long soak, this version of rice pudding can be made with long-, medium-, or short-grain brown rice. The softer the grain when it has finished cooking, the more pudding-like the consistency.

OIL: Almonds provide the oil in this dish, replacing the butter and milk in traditional recipes.

COOKING LIQUID: Almond milk makes a wholesome base for rice to dissolve into and become creamy. Nut milks tend to overflow a small pot, so allow plenty of head room for this expansive cooking liquid.

SWEETENER: Maple syrup and other liquid sweeteners like honey, rice syrup, and barley malt contribute liquid volume as well as sweetness. The flavors change drastically. Challenge your creativity with this dish: use butterscotch flavoring with barley malt in place of vanilla, or lemon with honey. You might need to change the oil when you change the sweetener and flavorings; for example, cashew milk feels more appropriate with butterscotch, and real butter with lemon and honey. Maybe hazelnut milk with rice syrup would be good. What do you think?

SPICES: Spices go well with sweet grain dishes. Cloves, cardamom, allspice, and nutmeg are other spices you might like to play with in this dish. A generous teaspoon of pure vanilla flavoring makes this all-time favorite combination of flavors complete.

SERVING SUGGESTIONS: I serve this as an in-between meal treat, not as a dessert. The combination of the complex sweetener, whole grain, and nut milk makes too sturdy a dish to close a meal. Serve this dish warm or chilled with fresh fruit sauce.

ALTERNATIVE
COOKING METHODS
NONE

Fresh Fruit Sauce

This sauce is intended to accompany the Sweet Almond Rice Pudding. It's really too sweet for any but dessert-style dishes.

1. Mix fruit juice and arrowroot flour in a saucepan and heat. Stir until thick and clear, then add fresh fruit and a pinch of sea salt.

¼ cup fruit juice
2 teaspoons arrowroot
  starch
2 cups fresh strawberries
Pinch of sea salt

Process

STYLE OF SAUCE: Clear sauce.
COOKING LIQUID: Apple juice is a standard ingredient for this kind of sauce, but I like to be very flexible, sometimes using mandarin orange, cherry, raspberry, or whatever lies in yonder refrigerator. A touch of liqueur perhaps?
BINDING AGENT: Kudzu starch can replace arrowroot for thickening and creating substance.
FRUIT: Raspberries, peaches, apricots, and blueberries are just a few other possible variations. Frozen fruit can replace fresh, but reduce the amount to 1½ cups or increase the arrowroot starch by ½ teaspoon. Taste the fruit and juice together before committing to the combination; some work together better than others.
SALT SEASONING: Stay with simple sea salt. This ingredient helps the flavors of the fruit come into the cooking liquid. It makes the sauce sweeter.

Basmati Rice With Pods and Color

3 cups water
Pinch of turmeric
1 teaspoon sea salt
1 teaspoon cardamom
  pods (whole cardamom)
1 teaspoon whole cloves
  (6 to 9)
1 teaspoon white or black
  ground pepper
2-inch piece cinnamon
  stick
1 bay leaf
1½ cups basmati brown
  rice, washed and
  drained
¾ cup fresh or frozen peas
¾ cup cooked diced
  carrots

This light and fluffy dish was created on a hot summer day. The color and aroma of rice steeped in fragrant golden liquid encouraged my appetite despite the heat, and got me thinking of all sorts of possibilities for quick second-stage dishes.

Yield: 4 cups (4–6 servings)

1. Combine water, turmeric, salt, and other spices in a heavy pot. Bring to a boil, add rice, cover, and reduce heat to medium-low. Steep until all the liquid is absorbed, about 45 minutes. Use a flame tamer to moderate heat.

2. Remove pods, cloves, and bay leaf. Mix in peas and carrots. Cover and let sit for 10 minutes before serving.

SERVING SUGGESTIONS: The presentation is light, airy, and summery. I like it with contrasting dollops of cold avocado sauce on the hot rice. It's also a great base for second-stage treatments like refrying and marinating.

Process

Pretreatment
SAUTÉ
First stage
STEEP
Second Stage
NONE

GRAIN: Basmati is only one choice for this dish. Others include Texmati, Lundberg Royal, long-grain brown, and even white rice. Quinoa, Job's tears, or millet will also work in this beautiful and fragrant dish.

COOKING LIQUID: Boiling the spices and leaves in water before adding the rice makes a flavored and colored cooking liquid, one of the most fun ways to vary first-stage grain dishes. Sometimes I use fresh garlic or ginger. Notice that the cooking liquid is hot when the grain meets the liquid. This helps to open the grain, making a slightly individual texture, more fluffy than sticky.

SALT SEASONING: Use plain sea salt, because there are so many other flavors going on. A salt seasoning with its own character would interfere, and possibly affect the color. The function of salt in this dish is simply to assist the first-stage method.

HERBS AND SPICES: The sweet spices chosen for this dish are based on Indian tradition, but then most sweet spices are. You might leave out the turmeric, as it affects only the color of the dish. Without it, a beautiful white background complements the decorative vegetables.

VEGETABLES: Peas and carrots, diced to match the size of the grain, spark the color of this dish. Sweet red pepper as a decorative accent, or black burdock (cooked, of course) will embellish it. Root vegetables need to be fairly well cooked when added to grain. I find the dish is more unified when cooked vegetables meet cooked grain, especially when the dish is served warm.

ALTERNATIVE COOKING METHOD: After boiling for a few minutes to establish the flavored cooking liquid, this dish can also be placed in the oven to bake, or pressure-cooked if you want a denser texture.

Basic Buckwheat Groats or Kasha

This is the basic first-stage preparation of buckwheat groats, either raw or dry-roasted (kasha). Which you use is a matter of taste. I almost always use kasha, but you may prefer the subtler flavor of the unroasted grain. Either way, this prepares the grain for second-stage methods including braising, deep-frying, refrying, and marinating. Or, you can serve it as is with a delicious sauce; Mushroom-Onion Sauce (p. 161) is my favorite.

2 cups vegetable stock
½ teaspoon vegetable salt
1 cup buckwheat groats, raw or dry-roasted

Yield: 4 cups (4–6 servings)

1. Bring stock to a slow boil. Add vegetable salt and buckwheat. Cover and steep for 20 minutes or until all liquid has been absorbed.

SERVING SUGGESTIONS: Serve warm with Mushroom-Onion Sauce, another clear sauce, or a flour or vegetable sauce.

Process

COOKING LIQUID: Chicken stock is a traditional alternative to vegetable stock. Water and vegetable bouillon also work. Experiment with the temperature of the cooking liquid; using cold liquid instead of hot changes the texture considerably (see Texture Chart, p. 20).
SALT SEASONING: Vegetable salt adds extra flavor, but sea salt would be fine. Think about how strong the cooking liquid is to determine which salt to use. A strongly flavored broth doesn't need a strong salt seasoning.

Pretreatment
NONE
First Stage
STEEP
Second Stage
NONE

ALTERNATIVE
COOKING METHODS
Pretreatment
DRY-ROAST
SAUTÉ
First Stage
BAKE

Amaranth Steeped in Beer and Rosemary

⅓ cup amaranth, washed
   and dry-roasted
⅔ cup beer
⅓ cup water
1 sprig fresh rosemary
Pinch of sea salt

"Joanne, what about amaranth?" asked my publisher, Linda Kramer. "Don't you cook with amaranth? It is one of our favorites." The last time I cooked with amaranth, at least ten years ago, my mouth felt like it was being torn apart. Now I realize that ten years ago cleaning amaranth was a primitive process. Taking up the challenge, I delved into "the creative process" to find a special combination of cooking liquids, seasonings, herbs, and other ingredients for a rebirth of this historic food.

Yield: 1⅓ cups (2–3 servings)

1. Combine beer, water, rosemary, and sea salt in a heavy pot. Cover and bring to a boil for about 5 minutes. Remove rosemary, add amaranth, cover, and reduce heat to medium-low. Steep until all the liquid is absorbed, about 35 minutes. Use a flame tamer to moderate heat.

TECHNIQUE NOTE: Save time by dry-roasting the amaranth while the cooking liquid is boiling.

SERVING SUGGESTIONS: Because there isn't any oil in this first-stage preparation, my first choice is to serve it with a luscious, rich nut sauce. A flour sauce, bean sauce, or vegetable sauce would also be possible. Amaranth is full of protein, so a vegetable sauce or flour sauce full of vegetables would be a good choice for a simple meal. If you choose a nut sauce or bean sauce, you will need a vegetable dish in the meal.

Process

Pretreatment
DRY-ROAST
First Stage
STEEP
Second Stage
NONE

GRAIN: The tiny little black seeds that spot a supply of amaranth are very bitter. It is hard to pick them out, so be aware of cooking with the bitterness. Dry-roasting is optional in this dish. Without it you will get a mass of glutinous grains prepared to hold a form and receive a hot sauce.

COOKING LIQUID: Because of the strong flavor of amaranth, I have chosen a strongly flavored cooking liquid to match it. Starting with a hot cooking liquid gives a less sticky texture. You can create variety in color and flavor by adding coloring agents like turmeric or beet juice, or herbs and spices.

SALT SEASONING: A pinch of plain sea salt assists the grain to receive the flavors of the cooking liquid. Vegetable salt would be good here; save other salt seasonings for second-stage cooking methods.
HERBS AND SPICES: Other strong seasonings such as sage, garlic, or cinnamon (not all together) could replace the rosemary.

ALTERNATIVE
COOKING METHODS
Pretreatment
SOAK
First Stage
BAKE

Sunflower Orange Sauce

These proportions make a medium-thick sauce. To adjust the substance, add a cooking liquid such as orange juice, mirin, or water to thin, or blend in nut butter and miso to thicken.

Yield: 2 cups (4–6 servings)

6 tablespoons sunflower
   butter
4 tablespoons light barley
   miso
1 cup orange juice
1 cup water
1 tablespoon minced
   orange zest

1. Blend sunflower butter and miso together. Work in orange juice and water to make a soupy texture.

2. Heat over medium-high heat, stirring, until thick. Lower heat and simmer for 10 minutes with flame tamer. Stir in orange zest.

SERVING SUGGESTIONS: This sauce was first created to go with Sweet and Festive Oats, but any first-stage cooked grain will do. Watch out for grain dishes with vegetables, as fruit and vegetable flavors do not always harmonize.

Process

STYLE OF SAUCE: Nut sauce.
BINDING AGENT: Sunflower butter. Normally I dislike sunflower oil and, by extension, sunflower butter; but cooked with orange juice and a strong flavored miso, it makes this a delicious sauce.
COOKING LIQUID: You could use full-strength orange juice for a stronger orange flavor and a somewhat sweeter sauce.
SALT SEASONING: Any miso works with this sauce, but I chose a fairly dark barley miso to match the rich brown color of the sunflower butter.
HERBS AND SPICES: Orange zest (the colored, oil-rich outer peel of an organic orange) embellishes both the flavor and the texture of the sauce.

Sweet and Festive Oats

3½ cups water
⅓ cup raw cashews
1 cup steel-cut or whole oats, washed and dry-roasted
¼ teaspoon sea salt
1 teaspoon allspice
½ teaspoon nutmeg
1½ tablespoons orange zest, minced

Oats like sweet flavors. Especially with nut milk as a cooking liquid, this dish feels like a festive pudding. Steeping is a standard cooking method, but using nut milk is not. Watch out for overflow if your pot isn't large enough. Use a 2-quart pot with a heavy lid that can create a good seal and a flame tamer to prevent scorching. Every bit of moisture is needed when using nut milk as a cooking liquid.

Yield: 3 cups (4–6 servings)

1. Blend cashews and water in blender for at least 1 minute to make cashew milk.

2. Combine oats, cashew milk, sea salt, allspice, nutmeg, and orange zest in a heavy pot. Cover, bring to a slow boil, and reduce heat to medium-low. Steep until all the liquid is absorbed, about 35 minutes. Use a flame tamer to moderate heat.

SERVING SUGGESTIONS: Sunflower Orange Sauce (p. 103) was created to go with this dish. Serve hot for an elegant breakfast or brunch.

Process

Pretreatment
DRY-ROAST
First Stage
STEEP
Second Stage
NONE

GRAIN: Any form of oats will work for this dish. Even rolled oats would be good, but reduce the cooking liquid volume by ¾ to 1 cup. Other grains you might try with this are Job's tears, quinoa, rice, or millet.
COOKING LIQUID: Nut milk for first-stage methods needs to be made thinner than for sauces. If the nut element (oil) is too rich, the grains have difficulty opening. If using other grains, check the grain chart, and remember to use ¼ cup more nut milk per cup of dry grain than you would other liquids.
OIL: Cashew nuts provide oil, replacing milk and butter in traditional pudding-style dishes.

ALTERNATIVE
COOKING METHOD
NONE

HERBS AND SPICES: Sweet, aromatic flavors such as allspice, nutmeg, and orange zest put a nice twist on this grain dish. Cardamom is another potential flavor to use in addition to the others or in place of nutmeg.

Pressure-Cooking

Pressure-cooking is usually thought of as a timesaving method. But for grain, I think of it more as a way to create a very special, dense texture and energetic value.

Contrary to some thinking, pressure-cooking is not dangerous, does not blast the food apart, and does not destroy nutritional value through the intensity of the process. The energetics remind me of springtime, when the energy bursting through the earth has to be strong. Spring brings intense penetration. Not all healing foods are gentle.

The beauty of this method is that all the energy is pressed inward as opposed to baking, boiling, and steeping, where the energy unfolds outward. Pressure-cooking is the first-stage method I choose to cook grain when my personal energy is all over the place. The concentrated feeling of grains pressed together gives me a sense of inward strength and confidence. Notice that the chart of first-stage cooking methods (p. 74) gives a wide range of times for pressure-cooking. The longer grain cooks, the more fire energy it stores.

PROCEDURE

- Measure, wash, and drain grain.
- Measure cooking liquid (see chart on p. 74) and combine grain, liquid, and a pinch of sea salt in the pressure cooker. Don't fill the pot more than two-thirds full.
- Make sure the seal is in place inside the rim of the lid of the cooker; line the lid up with the pot for easy fastening; confirm the weight on the valve if your cooker has one.
- On the highest heat, bring the pressure up in the cooker quickly. Pressure is up when the weight jiggles and hisses or, on some styles of cookware, when the indicator has risen. On occasion, I choose to let the grain cook on high heat for a few minutes before lowering the heat, to give the dish extra fire energy and to insure that the grains will stick together. A larger quantity of grain and liquid will take longer to reach the pressure point.
- When you have determined that the pressure has risen sufficiently in the cooker that it will endure the length of your desired cooking time, reduce the heat and begin timing. For example, if you are cooking quinoa for only ten minutes in the cooker, it wouldn't be necessary to extend the time that the weight hisses before you turn the temperature down. However, if you want

a very dense millet or rice dish, and you are cooking a large quantity of grain (3 to 5 cups), you may wish to let the pressure build for up to five minutes before turning down the heat.

- Place a flame tamer (see Cookware, p. 185) between the pot and the fire to moderate the heat.

- Medium-low is a good temperature to maintain the pressure in the pot. Check the gauge or lightly touch the weight to check the pressure; the weight should hiss (or the safety release valve stay up, or the gauge register pressure; each model is slightly different, so read the manufacturer's instructions).

- Sometimes the pressure comes down before the end of the timed cooking period. Do not try to bring the pressure back up again unless you are willing to burn your grain; I have never seen this work. Use another first- or second-stage method to finish cooking the grain.

- At the end of the cooking time, you may bring the pressure down one of three ways:

  1. Remove the pot from the stove to cool down slowly. This is my usual choice unless I need to open it quickly.

  2. Carefully set the cooker in the sink and run cold water over the side of the pot opposite the handle (keep the water off the valve). Be cautious with enameled pots, which may not be able to stand quick cooling.

  3. For a quick release, carefully lift the weight part way off the stem (some styles have a press-release button that has the same effect). Caution: if the food is very wet, like soup, the liquid may spray all over. So when you lift the weight, do it slowly and beware of a stream of hot steam shooting out.

- Opening the cooker should be easy once the pressure is down. Most modern cookers won't open if there is any pressure remaining in the pot. Jiggle the weight, and touch the safety valve to release any extra steam. Then slide the lid to open the pot. It is dangerous to open the cooker by force. If food has jammed the seal, remove it, clean it carefully without stretching it out. If the seal is old or cracking, rub a very small amount of oil around the seal before returning it to the pot.

Each brand of pressure cooker is unique. Follow the manufacturer's instructions carefully.

PRESSURE-COOKING:
To cook in a sealed pot that creates steam under pressure.

ENERGETICS:
Intense strength coming from very gentle, enduring steadfastness.

TEXTURE:
Each grain opens and clings to its neighbor, creating a chewy, somewhat sticky texture.

FLAVOR:
Natural flavor of the grain is enhanced.

COMPATIBLE COOKING METHODS:
All pretreatments and second-stage cooking methods; grains may be too sticky to absorb marinades. Hot sauces are great with this method.

Party Rice

This easy, attractive dish is elegant when shaped and served with hazelnut sauce. To shape a hot grain dish, press the mixture into lightly oiled forms. A serving bowl or individual custard cups work well.

Yield: 4 cups (4-6 servings)

1. Combine rice, water, and sea salt in a pressure cooker. Seal and bring up to pressure over high heat. Begin timing at this point, and reduce heat to medium-low (a flame tamer is required). Cook for 45 minutes.

2. While rice cooks, heat a skillet, add oil, and sauté burdock and carrots, sealing them one at a time. Cook with a pinch of sea salt until they are sweet and soft. Season with mirin, vinegar, and tamari.

3. When rice is done, remove pot from heat to cool slowly and release pressure according to manufacturer's instructions. Mix peas and cooked vegetables into hot rice. Cover pot again to steam peas for a few minutes before serving

SERVING SUGGESTIONS: Any sauce goes well with party rice. Meal companions would be soup and salad with a vegetable protein in either one.

2 cups short-grain brown rice, washed and drained
3 cups water
1 teaspoon sea salt
1 tablespoon dark sesame oil
1 burdock root, thinly sliced
1 carrot, diced medium
Pinch of sea salt
½ cup green peas, fresh or frozen
1 tablespoon mirin
½ tablespoon rice vinegar (optional)
Tamari or shoyu to taste
Parsley or fresh dill as garnish

Process

GRAIN: Short-grain brown rice has a distinct character that is enhanced by pressure-cooking. Other grains that can use this same process are millet, quinoa, oats, and Job's tears.

COOKING LIQUID: Water keeps the feeling of rice as a pure food. Rice cooked this way makes a great canvas for decorative vegetables and sauces and presents possibilities for second-stage cooking methods. Because of the intense energy of this cooking method, less cooking liquid is required than with other methods.

DECORATIVE VEGETABLES: Winter vegetables such as green onions, carrots, and burdock root should be cooked before they are mixed into the cooked grain. (Cooking the burdock dispels its powerful odor.) Summer vegetables such as corn, peas, and peppers can be steamed directly in the fresh pot of hot grain.

Pretreatment
NONE
First Stage
PRESSURE-COOK
Second Stage
NONE

ALTERNATIVE
COOKING METHODS
Pretreatment
DRY-ROAST
First Stage
STEEP
BAKE

Millet Mash

1 tablespoon light sesame oil
1 cup diced onion
1 cup fresh fennel, finely diced
1½ cups cauliflower
½ cup diced carrot (optional)
1 tablespoon fennel seeds, crushed
1 cup millet, washed and drained
3 cups water or vegetable broth
1 teaspoon vegetable salt

This is one of the best-known dishes of the macrobiotic diet, which avoids vegetables of the nightshade family. Taking the place of mashed potatoes, it replaces the vegetable with the power of millet.

I had been making this dish the same way for twenty years when one day, during class, a bulb of fresh fennel that was stored with the cauliflower fell out onto the cutting board. Pam asked if the fennel was going into the dish. "Why not?" What a great discovery. I love how the light but distinctive flavor of fennel permeates and matches the character of this dish.

Yield: 6 servings

1. Heat an uncovered pressure cooker over medium-high heat and add oil. Sauté onion, fennel, cauliflower, carrot, and fennel seeds, sealing them one at a time. Add the millet and stir occasionally for 2 minutes.

2. Add water or vegetable broth and vegetable salt. Seal and bring up to pressure. Begin timing at this point and adjust heat to maintain pressure (use a flame tamer). Cook for 20 minutes. Remove pot from heat to cool slowly; release pressure before opening.

SERVING SUGGESTIONS: Serve with a hot nut sauce or a not-too-thick bean or flour sauce. Or prepare with second-stage methods such as refrying, deep-frying, and, my favorite, braising.

Process

Pretreatment
NONE
First Stage
PRESSURE-COOK
Second Stage
NONE

GRAIN: Millet becomes a soft, moist, mashable dish when combined with cauliflower. The texture is soft and wet when the grain is hot and just cooked. It becomes drier and firmer as it cools.

COOKING LIQUID: Water will work if your taste buds are keen. But if you are serving this dish to people who are not accustomed to whole grain cookery, use a strong vegetable stock or bouillon.

OIL: Light sesame oil, olive oil, and ghee all harmonize with the lightness of this dish and the flavor of fennel that sings throughout.

SALT SEASONING: Vegetable salt adds to the flavor of the broth, but plain sea salt is a good choice also.

VEGETABLES: Cauliflower is the key vegetable in this dish because it can easily be mushy. Cut the vegetables small so that when they are cooked soft they can be blended into the grain with a wooden spoon. Squash, either winter or summer, would be a good alternative. Be prepared for the color to change if using an orange winter squash or a green summer squash. Decorative vegetables can be added before serving. Peas, for example, will cook in the steam of the hot grain.

Three-Grain Rice

In this dish, grains are the variables, not vegetables or herbs. Besides blending varieties of rice, you might try other combinations of grains: rice with millet, millet with quinoa, or Job's tears with teff. Or replace up to a quarter of the rice with whole oats, semipearled barley, or wheat. An elegant mixture of grains deserves a special presentation; press them into shapes before serving.

Yield: 4 cups (4–6 servings)

1. Wash and drain each rice separately.

2. Combine with water and salt in a pressure cooker. Seal and bring up to pressure over high heat. Begin timing at this point, and adjust heat to maintain pressure (a flame tamer is required). Cook for 45 minutes. Remove pot from heat to cool slowly; release pressure according to manufacturer's instructions before removing lid.

SERVING SUGGESTIONS: A hot vegetable, nut butter, bean, flour, or clear sauce would make this dish complete. I like to lay a portion of shaped grain onto the sauce and garnish with decorative vegetables.

Process

GRAIN: Specialty rice adds a spectacular dimension of color and taste to plain rice. Tones of purple emerge from this combination. Lundberg Farm sells several varieties of specialty rices already blended.
COOKING LIQUID: Plain water allows the individual flavors of the different grains to shine through and keeps the grain available for optional second-stage methods.
SALT SEASONING: Just sea salt, for the same reasons as plain water.

ALTERNATIVE
COOKING METHODS
First Stage
STEEP
BAKE

½ cup wild rice
1 cup short-grain brown
   rice
½ cup wehani rice
1 teaspoon sea salt
3 cups water

Pretreatment
NONE
First Stage
PRESSURE-COOK
Second Stage
NONE

ALTERNATIVE
COOKING METHODS
Pretreatment
DRY-ROAST
First Stage
STEEP
BAKE
BOIL
Second Stage
REFRY
BRAISE

Pressure-Cooked Sweet Brown Rice With Azuki Beans

½ cup azuki beans
Water to cover beans
2-inch piece kombu
1½ cups sweet brown rice
3 cups water or vegetable
    stock

This dish is an example of how to cook rice and beans together. Pressure-cooking accentuates the sticky character of sweet rice, and I find it essential to cooking beans and grain together in first-stage methods. No other method ensures that the beans are perfectly cooked and harmonious with the grains.

Actually, azuki beans are the only variety I cook together with grains in first-stage methods, because among all beans their carbohydrate content is closest to that of grains. Other beans have a stronger protein content, and they are best cooked separately and combined with grain in second-stage methods. You might try other beans such as lentils or black turtle or small red beans. Azuki beans will turn the whole dish deep purple, lentils a brownish green, and black or red beans, well, you can probably imagine what they will do. Only a small proportion of beans is needed, no more than 1 part beans to 4 parts grain.

Yield: 6–8 servings

1. Measure and wash grains and beans separately.

2. Cover beans with water in an uncovered pressure cooker and add kombu. Bring to a boil and cook rapidly, keeping a careful watch to prevent scorching, until water is gone. Immediately add 3 cups water or stock to beans and add rice.

3. Seal and bring up to pressure. Begin timing at this point, and adjust heat to maintain pressure (a flame tamer is required). Cook for 50 minutes. Remove from heat to cool slowly; release pressure according to manufacturer's instructions before removing lid.

SERVING SUGGESTIONS: The quickest way to season this dish is to sprinkle it with a cold dipping sauce of two parts tamari and one part tasty vinegar. For a more elegant presentation, serve a lovely hot sauce (vegetable, flour, clear, or nut) under or over molded individual servings of the grains and beans. Garnish with green onion, parsley, or sweet red pepper (consider mixing these decorative vegetables into the finished grain before pressing into shapes). For children, I make this dish into patties and pan-fry them. I call them "brain-burgers" because of the way they look, and tell the children that eating these will make them smart.

Process

GRAIN: Sweet rice is naturally sticky. I like the way it holds the beans. This works with other grains such as rice, millet, and Job's tears; see the grain chart on page 74 for amounts and cooking times. Be careful choosing beans for this first-stage combination. Long-cooking beans like garbanzos need to be soaked before boiling and need longer cooking before the grain is added. In step 2, cover the beans with 3 times their volume of water and cook until nearly dry.

COOKING LIQUID: Water is the safest liquid to use in this style of dish. It can be flavored with ginger or garlic, but avoid acid ingredients; the acid in vinegar or lemon juice will begin breaking down the beans too soon. In calculating the amount of cooking liquid for mixed grain and bean dishes, consider the volume of uncooked beans as if it were grain.

SALT SEASONING: First-stage cooking methods generally require a pinch of sea salt, but not when beans are in the pot. Salt inhibits the transformation of the bean to the smooth velvety quality it is known for, so don't add any salt until the beans are completely cooked. Serve with a sauce containing salt or prepare a second-stage method with a salt seasoning.

OIL: No oil. Again, a sauce or a second-stage method can supply oil. I like to braise this dish.

HERBS AND SPICES: Not necessary, but always possible. I like the plain flavor of this dish, and would prefer to save herbs and spices for a sauce or another part of the meal.

VEGETABLES: Depending on how you serve this dish, you may want to mix in some decorative vegetables, such as green onion, sweet red pepper, or parsley; or sauté major vegetables such as burdock root, carrot, or leek and mix them into the steaming pot of grain.

Pretreatment
NONE
First Stage
PRESSURE-COOK
Second Stage
NONE

ALTERNATIVE
COOKING METHODS
Pretreatment
SOAK
Second Stage
BRAISE

Sweet Brown Rice Mochi

2 cups sweet brown rice
3 cups water
½ teaspoon sea salt
1 teaspoon light sesame
   oil
1 tablespoon flour
   (preferably sweet rice
   flour, but any will do)

Soaking the grain is a labor-saving short cut in making mochi. The traditional method calls for pressure-cooking the sweet rice, pounding it, and letting it sit for a day or two to set up and ferment slightly. Pounding untreated grain takes great effort and it is even too stiff to put in a food processor. Soaking reduces both time and effort involved. If you don't have a pressure cooker, mochi can be made with steeped or baked rice; consult the grain chart on page 74 for adjustments in the cooking liquid and time.

Yield: 5 cups (6–8 servings)

1. Wash and drain sweet brown rice. Cover it with 3 cups water in the pressure cooker and soak for at least 6 hours.

2. Seal and bring up to pressure. Begin timing at this point and adjust heat to maintain pressure (use a flame tamer). Cook for 45 minutes. Remove pot from heat to cool slowly; release pressure according to manufacturer's instructions before removing lid.

3. Sprinkle salt over cooked grain and stir vigorously with a wooden mallet or pestle while the grain is still very hot. Continue until about 80 percent of the grains are broken. An alternative to the hand method is to wet a food processor with water or rub it with oil, and whiz the grain until it is smooth, wet, and sticky.

4. Rub an 8 × 8-inch baking dish with light sesame oil or ghee and dust it lightly with flour.

5. Lay the blended sweet rice in the floured pan. Let it set up for a few hours to overnight. Mochi is now ready to prepare in a second-stage method.

SERVING SUGGESTIONS: After it sets up in the pan, mochi can be cut into small cakes, to be served plain with a dipping sauce, dropped into soup, or cooked by a second-stage method. Braising, refrying, and deep-frying all bring flavors with them to make the dish complete. The most elegant way I have served this dish is deep-fried squares stuffed with cooked greens and scallions and covered with a pungent sauce.

Process

GRAIN: In Japanese tradition, this dish is made with white sweet rice. I like to make variations with ¼ part quinoa, teff, or amaranth.

COOKING LIQUID: Water is best, since the grain needs to soften and vegetable stock will break down easily as it soaks. You can flavor the cooking liquid just before cooking, with cinnamon stick for example.

SALT SEASONING: Unlike other first-stage rice dishes, no sea salt is cooked into the grain; instead, salt is added after cooking to assist the kernels in loosening their skins while you pound the hot grain. In partnership with pounding, the function of salt here is to help liquid pass through the cell walls, making a moist and broken grain.

HERBS AND SPICES: None in traditional mochi. Modern variations add flavorings like cinnamon, maple, vanilla, and seeds and nuts, which are pounded in in the final stage. For a savory variation, add chives and garlic while pounding. But my favorite way to play with the seasonings in this dish is in second-stage methods.

Pretreatment
SOAK
First Stage
PRESSURE-COOK
Second Stage
REFRY
DEEP-FRY
BRAISE

ALTERNATIVE
COOKING METHODS
NONE

Quinoa, Bean, and Vegetable Stew

1 tablespoon olive oil
1½ cups diced leek
½ cup diced carrot
½ cup diced zucchini
½ cup diced celery
¼ cup diced red or green
　　pepper
½ cup diced tomato
¼ cup minced cilantro
1 tablespoon dried
　　oregano leaves
2 tablespoons dried basil
　　leaves
2 tablespoons chili powder
1 cup quinoa, dry-roasted
2 cups red beans, cooked
　　soft
7 cups water
2 teaspoons vegetable salt
1 bay leaf
⅛ cup tamari
½ cup green beans
Fresh lime juice to taste

Pressure-cooking a stew is a short cut. The most important part of preparing this dish is sautéing the vegetables, herbs, and grain carefully. Sauté one vegetable at a time, sealing the cut edges so that they don't lose their identity in the broth. Sautéing is fundamental to creating a flavorful broth, because the juices from the vegetables and the hot oil create a concentrate of flavors that dissolve into the broth when cooking liquid is added. Take time to do this step. Long and slow sautéing creates a good stew.

Yield: 6–8 servings

1. Heat a heavy-bottomed pressure cooker over medium-high heat and add olive oil. Sauté vegetables, herbs, spices, and quinoa, sealing them one at a time.

2. Add beans, water, bay leaf, and vegetable salt. Seal pot and bring up to pressure. Begin timing at this point and adjust heat to maintain pressure. Use a flame tamer and cook 7 minutes. Bring pressure down quickly; add tamari and green beans. Let sit for 5 minutes. Serve with a squirt of fresh lime juice.

SERVING SUGGESTIONS: Croutons or corn chips add more grain to the dish. A salad completes this meal.

Process

Pretreatment
DRY-ROAST
First Stage
PRESSURE-COOK
Second Stage
NONE

GRAIN: Quinoa makes a quick soup. But millet is also a great possibility for this dish. Prepare dry-roasted grain for extra flavor.
COOKING LIQUID: Water extracts the flavors from twelve different vegetables and herbs. You could use a bit of vegetable juice, beer, or vegetable stock for an even richer flavor.
SALT SEASONING: Vegetable salt helps the broth arrive at its full flavor while it softens and sweetens the vegetables and grain. Tamari is a salt seasoning for adjusting the final flavor of the broth. Miso is an alternative. See the recipe for the millet stew on page 91.
OIL: Olive oil could be replaced by light sesame oil. Use enough to seal all the vegetables. Remember, this ingredient provides the vehicle for flavors to travel; be generous. You can use up to 3 tablespoons.

HERBS AND SPICES: I did not use garlic in this dish, but I know it would work. I must have been out of it that day. Cilantro and oregano are both strong herbs, and chili powder adds spice.

VEGETABLES: Unlike most of the grain dishes in this book, this dish depends on the strength of flavors and substance from vegetables. Even though it may look like I cleaned out my refrigerator on this dish, the vegetables were selected for their color, flavor, and compatibility of cooking time and character. Tomato, zucchini, green beans, and green pepper are summer foods; they cook within the same amount of time. A fall kaleidoscope of vegetables might include onion, burdock, butternut squash, celery, and red pepper.

The beans must be very well cooked before adding them to the stew. Small red, black turtle, garbanzo, pinto, or kidney beans should work equally well in this dish.

ALTERNATIVE
COOKING METHOD
First Stage
SLOW BOIL

Rice and Oats Together

1½ cups brown rice
½ cup oats, barley, or
   wheat berries
3 cups water
½ teaspoon sea salt

Bread grains are great in combination with dish grains. Cooking one part oats, barley, or wheat with three parts rice makes a great dish. I like to use the pressure-cooking method for this but steeping, baking, and all pretreatments are good possibilities. At least 2 cups of raw grain are needed for pressure-cooking; if you use other cooking methods, you can use less.

Yield: 6 cups (8–10 servings)

1. Wash and drain rice and oats.

2. Combine water, rice, oats, and salt in pressure cooker. Seal pot and bring up to pressure. Let cook for 1 minute before setting flame tamer in place and lowering heat to medium-low. Cook for 45 minutes.

3. Remove pot from heat to cool slowly; release pressure before removing lid. Mix grain thoroughly before serving.

SERVING SUGGESTIONS: Hot sauces such as nut butter, vegetable styles #1 and #2, clear sauce, bean sauce, or flour sauce all work beautifully on this simple first-stage dish.

Process

Pretreatment
NONE
First Stage
PRESSURE-COOK
Second Stage
NONE

ALTERNATIVE
COOKING METHODS
Pretreatment
DRY-ROAST
SAUTÉ
SOAK
First Stage
BAKE
STEEP
Second Stage
DEEP-FRY
BRAISE
REFRY

GRAIN: This method works for all grains except buckwheat. Quinoa with rice, teff with quinoa, and millet with Job's tears are other possible combinations.
COOKING LIQUID: Water is best for keeping the dish available to sauces and second-stage methods. However, you could flavor the water with ginger, garlic, or mint, or color it with turmeric for a gold shade or beet juice for pink.
SALT SEASONING: Sea salt is used for the same reason plain water is used.

Teff in Sweet Brown Rice

A small amount of teff gives a sweet, sorghumy flavor to a dish of brown rice, and the rice provides a vehicle for the tiny teff seeds. Steeping and baking will also work, but I like the way pressure-cooking enhances the texture of both grains.

If you soak the grains in cooking liquid and pound them together after cooking, you will have a lovely variation on mochi. The soaking and pounding also make the nutritional value of the teff seeds more available, because they are otherwise too small to chew.

1¾ cups sweet brown rice
¼ cup teff
3 cups water
½ teaspoon sea salt

Yield: 5 cups (6–8 servings)

1. Wash and drain grains.

2. Combine grains, water, and salt in a pressure cooker. Seal and bring up to pressure. Begin timing at this point and adjust heat to maintain pressure (use a flame tamer). Cook for 35 to 45 minutes. Remove pot from heat to cool slowly; release pressure according to manufacturer's instructions before removing lid.

SERVING SUGGESTIONS: Vegetable Velvet Sauce (p. 170) is excellent with this dish. The oil and sweet flavors from tempura vegetables are luscious against this beautifully plain grain.

Pretreatment
NONE
First Stage
PRESSURE-COOK
Second Stage
NONE

ALTERNATIVE
COOKING METHODS
Pretreatment
ALL
First Stage
BAKE
STEEP
Second Stage
BRAISE
RE-FRY
DEEP-FRY

Process

GRAIN: Brown teff adds speckles of color to glistening sweet rice, while white teff keeps the canvas open to possibilities. Any grain except buckwheat can be pressure-cooked. Look at the grain chart on page 74 for cooking liquid and time ratios.

COOKING LIQUID: I like to use water for this first-stage method because there are so many wonderful things to do with this dish in the second stage.

SALT SEASONING: Only sea salt for this first-stage cooking method.

Cooking Methods

Second-Stage

Braising, marinating, deep-frying, and refrying are what I call second-stage cooking methods. They are used to give additional flavors, colors or textures to grains cooked by first-stage methods. Think of these optional secondary treatments not as a way to cook "leftovers" but as a way to generate totally new dishes with new seasonings.

As already noted, second-stage methods depend for their success on specific textures created in the first stage. For example, marinated grain dishes need open, receptive grains to soak in the marinade; so choose first-stage preparations that create an open individual texture: dry-roasting, hot liquid, boiling, steeping, baking.

This stage of grain cookery is fun! Decorative vegetables and an array of seasonings visually and tastefully complete second-stage dishes. Given some first-stage grain around the kitchen to work with, you can create an endless variety of dishes quickly.

Braising

Braising, steeping food in seasoned liquid after it has been sealed in hot oil, is a delightful way to use precooked grain. Like the seasonings in a marinade, the flavors of the braising liquid permeate each grain. I usually combine a sour liquid and a salt seasoning in the braising liquid. Herbs, spices, and decorative vegetables round out the dish, but it can be quite good with the braising liquid alone. Choosing ingredients is a mix and match process; start with an oil for browning, or a cooking liquid, or a salt seasoning, and add compatible ingredients.

PROCEDURE

- Heat a skillet and coat it with oil, as if preparing to sauté. The more oil you use, the crustier the dish. If using vegetables and herbs, sauté them in the oil now.
- Add the cooked grain, coat it in the oil, cover it, and cook it over a medium fire.
- Mix the braising liquid (about one-third of the volume of grain) and pour it over the browned grain; cover the skillet immediately. A crust will form as it cooks if you don't stir the grain too often. For a bottom crust, after the grain has been sautéed, turn the grain infrequently.
- (Optional.) To braise in the oven, place the skillet (covered or uncovered) in the oven after adding the liquid and bake until liquid is absorbed.

BRAISING:
To steep a food in a seasoned liquid after it has been sealed in hot oil.
ENERGETICS:
Balanced between the dynamic energy of sautéing and refrying and calm and gentle steeping.
TEXTURE:
Moist.
FLAVOR:
Full of a combination of flavors depending on braising liquid, pretreatments, and first-stage liquids and seasonings.
COMPATIBLE COOKING METHODS:
All:

CREATING BRAISING LIQUIDS

Braising liquids are put together by choosing a combination of one or more of the following seasonings and cooking liquids. Mix and match the categories with the ratio of salt seasoning to liquid volume being about 1:7, or to taste. I usually think of braising liquids as a combination of sour and salty, but feel free to use other combinations, including sweet and sour, or sweet and salty along with fragrant herbs or pungent and sweet spices.

COOKING LIQUID	SALT SEASONING	HERBS	SPICES
Water	Sea salt	Arugula	Allspice
Juice	Miso	Basil	Caraway
Apple	Rice	Tarragon	Cardamom
Orange	Barley	Bay leaf	Cayenne pepper
Cranberry	Buckwheat	Chives	Chili powder
Lemon	Red, white, yellow	Cilantro	Chinese five spice
Stock	Chick-pea	Dill	Cinnamon
Nut milk	Tamari	Fennel	Cloves
Beer	Shoyu	Marjoram	Coriander
Wine	Umeboshi	Mint	Cumin
Sherry	Whole plum	Oregano	Ginger (fresh)
Mirin	Paste	Parsley	Garlic
Vinegar	Vinegar	Rosemary	Horseradish
Apple cider	Sauerkraut	Sage	Nutmeg
Rice	Vegetable salt	Thyme	Paprika
Wine			Pepper (black & white)
Umeboshi			
Raspberry			

Braised Millet in Umeboshi and Lemon

This dish is a standard in my family. I like it best at breakfast, where sour flavors prepare me better for a day of work than sweet flavors from traditional breakfasts.

1 to 2 tablespoons light
   sesame oil
¼ cup sliced green onions
2 cups cooked millet or
   Millet Mash (see p. 108)
2 tablespoons umeboshi
   vinegar
2 tablespoons lemon juice
2 tablespoons water

Yield: 2 cups (4 servings)

1. Heat a skillet over medium heat and add oil. Sauté onions and cooked millet for about 7 minutes or until they are slightly browned.

2. Mix vinegar, lemon juice, and water and pour over buckwheat. Cover and cook until liquid has been absorbed into the grain. Turn once.

SERVING SUGGESTIONS: Serve hot. Additional protein like tofu, tempeh, eggs, or smoked salmon and a vegetable dish will complete the meal.

Process

Pretreatment
NONE
First Stage
PRESSURE-COOK
Second Stage
BRAISE

GRAIN: Leftover Millet Mash is a perfect candidate for braising, as is any cooked millet dish on the dry side.

COOKING LIQUID: Try other braising liquid combinations, perhaps apple cider vinegar with red miso, or rice vinegar with tamari.

OIL: Any oil will do. If you like the taste of butter, try ghee.

SALT SEASONING: Umeboshi vinegar is not only the sour cooking liquid, but also the salt seasoning. When changing salt seasonings, make sure you replace the flavors with a sour cooking liquid.

VEGETABLE: A decorative vegetable adds color and flavor. Keep it simple; don't use more than three.

ALTERNATIVE
COOKING METHODS
Pretreatment
DRY-ROAST
First Stage
BAKE
STEEP
Second Stage
REFRY

Kasha and Cabbage
Braised in Sauerkraut Juice

**2 tablespoons light
sesame oil**
½ cup sliced green onions
1¾ cups red cabbage
3 cups cooked kasha
½ cup sauerkraut juice
¼ cup water (optional)

Yield: 3 cups (6 servings)

1. Heat a skillet over medium heat and add oil. Sauté onions, cabbage, and cooked kasha for about 7 minutes or until they are slightly browned.

2. Mix sauerkraut juice and water and pour over buckwheat and vegetables. Cover and cook until liquid has been absorbed into the grain. Turn once.

SERVING SUGGESTIONS: Serve hot for breakfast with tempeh bacon.

Process

Pretreatment
DRY-ROAST
First Stage
STEEP
Second Stage
BRAISE

ALTERNATIVE
COOKING METHODS
First Stage
BAKE
Second Stage
REFRY

GRAIN: Use dry-roasted buckwheat, cooked by baking or steeping. I have prepared this dish with rice and millet, and have a sense that Job's tears and quinoa would also be good.

COOKING LIQUID: The braising liquid for this dish relies on the juice in a sauerkraut jar. Press the sauerkraut away from the edge of the jar and the juice will rise. Water is optional; if you don't need to soften the grain, and you like the intensity of straight sauerkraut juice, don't use water.

OIL: Light sesame oil could just as well be olive or hazelnut oil.

SALT SEASONING: Sauerkraut juice is similar to umeboshi but is less intense. Other salt seasonings work with other cooking liquids. See the chart on creating braising liquids on page 120.

VEGETABLES: Green onion and red cabbage both act as decoration, but red cabbage doubles as a major vegetable. Try using green cabbage and red onion, or, better yet, try whatever is at hand.

Braised Job's Tears

Braising balances the density of Job's tears. Creating a crust from an inherently slippery grain is tricky, but it can be accomplished by long slow cooking on a medium flame without stirring.

Yield: 3 cups (4 servings)

1. Heat a skillet over medium heat and add oil. Sauté garlic, tarragon, green onion, red pepper, and cooked Job's tears for about 7 minutes.

2. Mix sauerkraut juice, umeboshi vinegar, and water and pour over Job's tears and vegetables. Cover and cook until liquid has been absorbed into the grain creating a crust. Turn once.

SERVING SUGGESTIONS: Garnish with tamari-roasted seeds or nuts, and serve with a vegetable salad or soup.

2 tablespoons olive oil
3 cloves fresh garlic, minced
6 tablespoons fresh tarragon
½ cup sliced green onion
½ cup diced sweet red pepper
3 cups cooked Job's tears
¼ cup sauerkraut juice
¼ cup umeboshi vinegar
¼ cup water

Process

GRAIN: Job's tears makes a great canvas for flavor and yet carries its own distinction. Pressure-cook or steep the grain with plain water in the first stage to keep the flavors clear.

COOKING LIQUID: The courage to combine sauerkraut juice and umeboshi in a braising liquid came from students Claire Zimmerman and Sherwood Stockwell during an improvisation session. They wanted to balance the nutty, thick, and slippery character of Job's tears with flavors that would cut through.

OIL: Olive oil carries the flavor of garlic and tarragon throughout the grain. Ghee and light sesame oil would also be good.

SALT SEASONING: Both umeboshi vinegar and sauerkraut juice are salt seasonings. You might want to adjust the end taste with a touch of tamari.

HERBS AND SPICES: Even though both are potent, garlic and tarragon are subtle against the strong braising liquid flavors. With cooking time, all these flavors blend together.

VEGETABLES: Green onions and sweet red pepper brighten the plain white beads as decorative vegetables. Leeks, black olives, and cooked carrots are other options.

Pretreatment
NONE
First Stage
PRESSURE-COOK
Second Stage
BRAISE

ALTERNATIVE
COOKING METHODS
First Stage
BAKE
STEEP
BOIL
Second Stage
REFRY

Kasha and Brussels Sprouts Braised With Umeboshi Vinegar

1 tablespoon toasted
  sesame oil
½ cup sliced onions
Pinch of crushed cara-
  way or fennel seeds
  (optional)
¾ cup brussels sprouts,
  quartered
1 cup cooked buckwheat
  groats
⅛ cup umeboshi vinegar
1 tablespoon fresh lemon
  juice
⅛ cup water

Compare this braised buckwheat dish with Kasha and Cabbage Braised in Sauerkraut Juice (p. 122). Notice the difference in texture and taste between buckwheat and kasha and the softer flavor of sauerkraut juice in the braising liquid.

Another favorite grain for this treatment is millet. Try it with Millet Mash (p. 108), with or without the brussels sprouts.

Yield: 3 servings

1. Heat a skillet over medium heat and add oil. Sauté onions, seeds, brussels sprouts, and cooked buckwheat in sesame oil for about 7 minutes or until sprouts are bright green and grain is lightly browned.

2. Mix vinegar, lemon juice, and water and pour over grain and sprouts. Cover and cook until liquid has been absorbed into grain. Turn once.

SERVING SUGGESTIONS: I like this dish as a hearty cool-weather breakfast, perhaps with a poached egg or tempeh bacon on the side. It is great for any meal, but is best served warm.

TECHNIQUE NOTE: By not using a cover after you add the braising liquid, you create a deliciously crusty dish. If it becomes too crusty, cover the skillet for a minute or three and the crust will steam off the bottom.

Process

Pretreatment
NONE
First Stage
STEEP
Second Stage
BRAISE

GRAIN: Unroasted buckwheat is fairly slippery, so you may prefer to do this dish with kasha. Prepare either form of buckwheat by steeping. This dish will work with any grain. The texture is not especially important, but when grain is dry, the braising liquid enlivens the flavor and the texture.

OIL: Any oil will do. Ghee or butter is delicious. But dark sesame oil lends an additional flavor that is rarely surpassed. The more oil you use to brown this dish, the crustier and more sensual it will be.

HERBS AND SPICES: Caraway and fennel seeds are simply suggestions. One, none, or a different flavor may be used. The vegetables, grain, oil and braising liquid can carry this style of dish alone.

VEGETABLES: Braising green vegetables always raises the danger of turning them brown. When cooking with vinegar and other acid formulas, know that there is a 90 percent chance that the green of the vegetable may turn brown. The taste is delicious; but if you want to capture the bright green color, make sure the vegetables are perfectly cooked before you add the braising liquid, reduce the amount of water in the braising liquid, and serve the dish within 1 minute of applying the braising liquid.

COOKING LIQUID: Lemon juice, water, and umeboshi vinegar compose the braising liquid, supplying both sour and salty flavors. You can substitute other blends such as miso, water, and rice vinegar, or tamari, lemon, and water.

ALTERNATIVE
COOKING METHODS
Pretreatment
DRY-ROAST
First Stage
BAKE
Second Stage
REFRY

Braised Mediterranean Oats

This is an example of what you can do with oats besides breakfast oatmeal. Change the ingredients to suit your foods at hand.

Yield: 2 cups (4–6 servings)

1 tablespoon olive oil
1 tablespoon oregano, crushed
⅓ cup sliced green onions
⅓ cup diced carrot
¼ cup chopped black olives
2 cups cooked whole oats
⅛ cup balsamic vinegar
⅛ cup red wine or marsala
½ teaspoon sea salt
Water
¼ cup parsley, for garnish

1. Heat a skillet over medium-high heat and sauté oregano, green onions, carrot, olives, and cooked oats, sealing them one at a time. Cook until vegetables are partially cooked and oats are slightly brown.

2. In a measuring cup, combine vinegar, wine, and salt and water to total ⅓ cup liquid. Pour liquid over grain and cook, uncovered, until liquid has disappeared. Don't stir if you want a crusty bottom; just turn once halfway through the cooking. Mix in parsley before serving.

SERVING SUGGESTIONS: Serve hot, with a vegetable protein dish and a simple vegetable.

Process

GRAIN: Bake oats to prepare them for braising. Rice, millet, quinoa, or Job's tears would be good alternative grains for this dish.

COOKING LIQUID: Oats call for a strong braising liquid to cut through the natural fat of the oat groat. Balsamic vinegar (one of the most distinctive vinegars) and wine give this grain a kick.

OIL: Olive oil is most compatible here, but any oil will do in a pinch

SALT SEASONING: Sea salt keeps it simple, but diluted miso and tamari would also be options for the braising liquid.

HERBS AND SPICES: Use oregano, but garlic and other herbs also work.

VEGETABLES: Sweet red pepper could replace carrots as a decorative vegetable; it cooks more quickly than carrots.

Pretreatment
NONE
First Stage
BAKE
Second Stage
BRAISE

ALTERNATIVE
COOKING METHODS
Pretreatment
DRY-ROAST
First Stage
STEEP
PRESSURE-COOK
BOIL

Braised Eggplant and Quinoa

8 slices eggplant
3 to 6 tablespoons dark
 sesame oil
¼ cup tamari
¼ cup rice vinegar
½ cup water
3 tablespoons sake or
 mirin
1 teaspoon ginger juice
 (see p. 83)
1 teaspoon minced garlic
4 cups cooked quinoa
½ cup diced red pepper

Braised eggplant is so lusciously delicious I had to find a way to share it with you. The quinoa is not exactly braised, but the eggplant has an abundance of braising liquid, which soaks into the grain. This can be cooked on the stove or in the oven; I usually use the oven because I can make a larger quantity.

Yield: 4 to 6 servings

1. Heat a large skillet over medium heat and add oil. Brown eggplant on each side, adding more oil as needed. Leave the eggplant in the skillet or place a single layer in a 9 × 13-inch baking dish.

2. Mix together tamari, vinegar, water, mirin, ginger juice, and garlic. Pour over eggplant, cover, and bake in a preheated 350°F oven for about 15 minutes. Turn eggplant over, remove cover, and cook for another 15 minutes or until liquid has cooked into eggplant and it is very soft and moist. (If eggplant has finished cooking and liquid remains, use the liquid to season the quinoa.)

3. Mix cooked quinoa and red pepper and press into the baked eggplant. Serve by inverting onto a plate, eggplant on top of quinoa.

SERVING SUGGESTIONS: Serve with a hearty bean soup and a green salad.

Process

Pretreatment
NONE
First Stage
STEEP
Second Stage
BAKE/BRAISE

GRAIN: This dish is also excellent with rice or millet. The texture of the grain is not too important for this dish. If you have leftover first-stage grain, serving it in this manner will refresh it. If you are cooking grain for this dish, the texture can be either dry or moist.
COOKING LIQUID: Raspberry vinegar is a nice alternative to rice vinegar, especially when used with miso. Or try umeboshi vinegar, either on its own or mixed with lemon or lime juice.
SALT SEASONING: Tamari can be replaced with miso. If using umeboshi in place of rice vinegar, remember that it supplies salt too.
OIL: Dark sesame oil completes the traditional flavors of the braising liquid. Light sesame oil would be a second choice. Olive oil would be good if you eliminate the ginger, replacing it with tarragon or fennel.
HERBS AND SPICES: Garlic and ginger are best. A heavy dose of fennel, tarragon, or cardamom could be alternatives.

ALTERNATIVE
COOKING METHOD
NONE

Braised Teff With
Miso and Wine Vinegar

My father used to serve us cream of wheat with slices of sharp cheddar cheese. I know that dairy foods are not part of this book, and this dish will stand on its own without the cheese, but I do suggest you try it with cheese; it's a perfect match. I like to braise teff because the flavors of a braising liquid cut through the sweet, glutinous character of the grain.

Yield: 1½ cups (2–4 servings)

1 tablespoon light sesame oil
½ cup minced onion
½ cup minced zucchini
¼ cup cilantro leaves (optional)
1½ cups cooked teff
2 tablespoons white wine vinegar
1 tablespoon white miso
Water

1. Heat a skillet over medium-high heat and add oil. Sauté onions, cilantro, and cooked teff, sealing them one at a time. Cook until vegetables are partially cooked and teff is slightly brown.

2. In a measuring cup, dilute miso in vinegar and enough water to total ¼ cup liquid. Pour liquid over grain and cook, uncovered, until liquid has disappeared. Don't stir if you want a crusty bottom; just turn once about halfway through the cooking.

SERVING SUGGESTIONS: Serve hot, with major vegetable dishes.

Process

GRAIN: Steeped teff reminds me of Wheatena, only its wholeness comes through energetically with more taste, character, and power.
COOKING LIQUID: The water in either the first stage or the braising liquid can be replaced with another cooking liquid, such as vegetable stock or flavored water.
OIL: I prefer light sesame oil in this dish because it doesn't interfere with the sweetness of teff. Other oils with more flavor will also work; just be aware of what flavors you are working with.
SALT SEASONING: White miso accents the sweetness of this grain. Try umeboshi vinegar or tamari for a sharper taste.
HERBS AND SPICES: Cilantro (fresh coriander) is a strong flavor common in Mexican dishes. Also known as Chinese parsley, this herb spikes Chinese soups and other dishes.
VEGETABLES: Teff is so very small that you need to cut the onion and zucchini into very small cubes so that they blend in. Other vegetables can also be good for this dish. Just make sure they are cut small, and cooked well.

Pretreatment
NONE
First Stage
STEEP
Second Stage
BRAISE

ALTERNATIVE
COOKING METHODS
Pretreatment
SOAK
DRY-ROAST
First Stage
BAKE
BOIL
Second Stage
REFRY
MARINATE

Deep-Frying

Deep-frying creates some of the most satisfying grain dishes possible. Grain is so plain and bland it rarely has an opportunity to show off. But when formed into croquettes and fried until crisp on the outside, whole grains become a delightful sensual morsel. When done properly, deep-frying does not produce greasy food. A cold dipping sauce full of pungent, sour, and salty flavors cuts through the small amount of oil remaining in the food, aiding digestibility as well as balancing the taste.

The success of deep-frying depends on the texture of the grain, which is determined in the first-stage cooking method. Pressure-cooking gives the most cohesive grain; baked and steeped grains are also workable.

PROCEDURE

- Have a bowl of water to wet your hands while shaping the grain. Moisten your hands just enough to avoid having the grain stick to you, but not so much as to add extra liquid to the finished product.
- Determine whether the grain will need additional binding ingredients. If the grain is too dry the croquette will fall apart when you hold it between two fingers and press lightly. If it is too wet, it will not hold a shape. Balance a too-dry texture by adding a slight amount of water and a light dusting of flour; balance wet grain by adding a slight amount of flour, or, if possible, more cooked grain (even if it is a different kind). Too much added flour and water will make a gooey, not chewy, croquette.
- Add decorative vegetables and seasonings to taste. Form the grain into a firm shape by pressing a small handful of grain together firmly into flat, round, triangular, or log shapes. The edges must be tightly packed. Draw on your snowball making experience.
- (Optional.) For an extra sealing crust, roll your croquettes in fine grain flour, bread crumbs, or a combination of the two. Whole-wheat pastry, quinoa, and corn flours are very fine and may be seasoned with herbs and spices. Avoid salt and sweeteners as they attract too much oil. These flavors can be added to the dipping sauce if needed.
- Prepare a plate with paper towels as a place to drain the hot croquettes.

- Heat the oil in a wok or deep skillet to 375 to 400°F. Use a base of safflower oil, 2 to 4 inches deep. You may add up to 10 percent sesame, coconut, peanut, or corn oil for flavor, but these oils (if they are expeller pressed) cannot get as hot as needed for this cooking method. They will boil over the side, making a dangerous mess if you use too much of any one of them. When the oil is too cool, less than 375°F, croquettes will come out soggy and oily. When the temperature of the oil gets too hot (more than 400°F), the outside will cook too quickly and might burn without cooking the inside of the croquette.
- If you don't have an oil thermometer, look at the oil for clues to its temperature. The oil is ready when wavy lines move quietly across the top like the gentle ripples from the moment a gnat hits the water of a quiet pond. The faster the lines move the hotter the oil. If the oil starts to smoke it is getting too hot (over 400°F). To test for readiness, drop a small piece (a few grains) of the grain mixture into the hot oil. If it sinks to the bottom and stays there, the oil is too cold; it will quickly jump to the top if the oil is ready.
- Carefully lower the croquettes into the oil. The oil should receive the croquette and surround it with many active little bubbles of oil. Cook the croquettes evenly on both sides until crisp outside and hot inside (they are usually done when the bubbles quiet down). You can feel the crispness of the outer crust with chopsticks, or an oil skimmer.
- Each time you add a croquette the oil will cool off. It is easier to maintain the temperature of the oil by adding food instead of changing the amount of fire. However, too many croquettes added at once will lower the temperature too far and possibly cause the oil to overflow.
- Drain the cooked croquettes on a paper towel. They may be kept in a slow (300°F) oven for up to half an hour without losing too much of their character, but they are best served hot, directly from the oil.
- After cooking, let the oil cool and strain it into a jar through a cheesecloth-lined funnel (to remove burnt pieces of food). Store in the refrigerator. I use this oil many times until it gets too low or dark, at which point it makes the best popcorn ever.

DEEP-FRYING:
To cook grain by submerging clusters of it in hot oil (375 to 400°F) until they are golden and crusty.

ENERGETICS:
Extreme heat and very fast, like boiling in oil.

TEXTURE:
Crunchy and crisp on the outside, chewy on the inside.

FLAVOR:
Depends on the kind of oil, the grain, seasonings, and decorative vegetables mixed into the grain before cooking.

COMPATIBLE COOKING METHODS:
Pressure-cook, steep, bake; use cold liquid and cold grain.

Deep-Fried Rice Croquettes

2 cups cooked rice
3 tablespoons lemon zest,
minced
1 green onion, minced
Safflower oil for deep-
frying

DIPPING SAUCE
1 tablespoon tamari or
shoyu
1 teaspoon mirin
1 teaspoon rice vinegar

This and the following two recipes give you an idea of the options in deep-fried grain dishes, with differences in the choice of grain, the shape of the pieces to be fried, and the dipping sauce. They are basically interchangeable. Make sure you read the previous pages for pointers on the deep-frying technique.

Yield: 4 to 6 croquettes (2–3 servings)

1. Mix grain with lemon zest and onion. Combine dipping sauce ingredients in a separate bowl.

2. Press a small handful of grain together as if you were making a snowball. Flatten slightly and smooth out the edges by rotating the ball in the palm of your hand. Always press toward center.

3. Heat 2 to 3 inches of oil in a wok or deep skillet to 375 to 400°F. Make sure there is at least 1 inch from the top of the pot to the top of the oil so there will be room for adding several croquettes at a time. When the lines are wavy, test the oil with a piece of rice. If it rebounds off the bottom quickly, add a few croquettes slowly to the oil.

4. Fry croquettes a few at a time until golden brown on both sides. Drain well and serve hot with dipping sauce.

SERVING SUGGESTIONS: Serve the croquettes hot, right out of the pot as an appetizer or snack. A salty and pungent dipping sauce cuts through the oil and balances the flavor. These crispy chews are also good in vegetable soup or stew or as a cold-morning breakfast.

Process

Pretreatment
NONE
First Stage
PRESSURE-COOK
Second Stage
DEEP-FRY

GRAIN: The grain needs to hold together by itself as it can. Short-grain brown rice is best; other rice, as long as it sticks together, will also be good. Millet and buckwheat love this deep-frying method. **COOKING LIQUID:** No liquids should be added after the first stage. If you do need to add liquid to the grain before deep-frying, use water. Sweet or salty ingredients attract too much oil. However, in the dipping sauce, play fully with a variety of cooking liquids: lemon juice in place of vinegar, ginger juice water, beer, etc. **OIL:** Safflower is the best oil for deep-frying. You can use up to 10 percent of other oils like sesame or peanut if they are unrefined. But any more will make the cooking difficult. (The only reason I would combine oils is if I were short on volume and needed oil to fill the pot.)

SALT: Salt comes in the dipping sauce. Since salt attracts oil, don't add any extra to the croquettes before frying.

HERBS AND SPICES: Save them for other parts of the meal, or perhaps put one in the dipping sauce. Lemon provides enough flavoring here.

VEGETABLES: You could add a small amount of a decorative vegetable like green onion or parsley.

ALTERNATIVE
COOKING METHODS
First Stage
STEEP

Deep-Fried Kasha Croquettes

This is an exquisite way to present kasha. Dry-roasted buckwheat loves oil, and even people who don't care too much for buckwheat have enjoyed these morsels.

Yield: 6 to 8 croquettes or 20 balls (3–4 servings).

1. Shape cooked kasha into little balls or croquettes. Make sure they will hold together. Adjust the texture if necessary (see p. 128). Combine dipping sauce ingredients in a separate bowl.

2. Heat 2 to 3 inches of oil in a wok or deep skillet to 375 to 400°F. Fry the croquettes a few at a time, cooking on both sides until crisp. Remove and drain on paper towels. Serve hot with dipping sauce.

SERVING SUGGESTIONS: These morsels can be an appetizer, a main course, or dumplings for soup or stew. I like them best served hot with dipping sauce. If not serving immediately, keep them warm in an oven for up to 20 minutes at 250 to 300°F.

3 cups cooked kasha
½ cup minced white onion
½ cup minced parsley
Safflower oil for frying

DIPPING SAUCE
2 tablespoons tamari or
shoyu
½ **tablespoon vinegar**
½ **tablespoon lemon juice**
½ **teaspoon ginger juice**
(optional)

Process

GRAIN: This can also be made with raw buckwheat groats, giving a slight variation in flavor. Actually, you can use any grain that can hold together in hot oil.

OIL: See page 129.

HERBS AND SPICES: You can mix herbs and spices such as garlic powder or crushed caraway seeds into the grain before shaping, or you can jazz up the dipping sauce.

VEGETABLES: Onions, peppers, and squash are just a few possibilities. Whatever you use, cut it small so it doesn't break up the form of the croquette.

Pretreatment
DRY-ROAST
First Stage
STEEP
Second Stage
DEEP-FRY

ALTERNATIVE
COOKING METHOD
Second Stage
BRAISE

Millet Sticks

1 cup millet
3 cups cold water
1 teaspoon vegetable salt
½ cup minced or grated
   onion
Safflower oil for frying

DIPPING SAUCE
2 tablespoons shoyu
1 tablespoon rice vinegar

I like to make these sticks as thin as possible. They remind me of French fries, but I call them "light sabers" as they are quite firm, crispy, and radiant. I frequently pressure-cook the millet in the first stage of this dish to ensure that the grains will be firm enough to deep-fry. If you do pressure-cook, use only 2¾ cups water instead of 3 cups.

Yield: 6 servings

1. Wash and drain millet. Steep it in water with vegetable salt for 40 minutes.

2. Mix in onion. Press into a 9 × 13-inch baking pan or onto a cookie sheet. Let cool to room temperature. Combine dipping sauce ingredients in a separate bowl.

3. Cut into French-fry-size strips or other shapes. Let dry a bit, or roll in flour for a drier surface.

4. Heat 2 to 3 inches of oil in a wok or deep skillet to 375 to 400°F. Deep-fry millet sticks a few at a time until golden brown. Serve hot with dipping sauce or ketchup.

SERVING SUGGESTIONS: Serve hot with dipping sauce as a main dish, an appetizer, or a companion to soup.

Process

Pretreatment
NONE
First Stage
STEEP
Second Stage
DEEP-FRY

GRAIN: The grain for this presentation needs to be firm enough to hold its shape. Millet has the best character for making these thin sticks.
COOKING LIQUID: Plain water is best for the first-stage method. Vegetable stock will work if it doesn't have oil in it.
OIL: See page 129.
SALT SEASONING: As in all deep-fried grain dishes, save the salt seasonings for the dipping sauce to avoid attracting excess oil into the grain.
HERBS AND SPICES: Millet is very bland; anything is possible here. I have used chili powder, paprika, and garlic powder for variety.
VEGETABLES: Minced onion boosts the flavor of this bland grain. If you grate an onion to onion juice, the light sabers are less likely to fall apart. Parsley, green onion, or green pepper minced very fine would be good decorative vegetables.

ALTERNATIVE
COOKING METHODS
NONE

Refrying

Refrying is a very quick method of preparing grain dishes, best represented by the familiar "fried rice." In this method, small cut (diced) vegetables and herbs or spices are added to flavor the oil, which carries the flavors and coats the grain. A salt seasoning adds the finishing touch.

Although some fat is necessary for refrying, the amount of fat you use is variable. If you are on a lean diet or other dishes in the meal contain fat, you may want to use less oil; in cold, windy weather more oil may be desired.

Oil is necessary for the function of carrying flavors around the grain. Strong-flavored oils such as dark sesame, corn, olive, or hazelnut make a contribution to the taste of the dish, as well as the function. Mild flavored oils like safflower or canola perform only in function. I like to use ghee for its special buttery taste and the fine crust it makes.

PROCEDURE

- Heat skillet; add oil, spices or herbs, and vegetables. (Remember, a warm skillet needs less oil.)
- Cook the vegetables until they are two-thirds cooked, stir in the grain, and continue cooking uncovered until the vegetables are done and the grain has integrated with the oil and seasonings.

REFRYING:
To heat cooked grain in an oiled skillet, usually with vegetables and salt seasonings.

ENERGETICS:
Quick, light fire.

TEXTURE:
Soft, somewhat individual, not too wet.

FLAVOR:
Depends on vegetables, oil, and salt seasonings.

COMPATIBLE COOKING METHODS:
All pretreatments and first-stage cooking methods.

Refried Amaranth

**2 teaspoons sesame oil
1 clove garlic, minced
1 green onion, slivered
1 small zucchini, diced
¼ cup diced red pepper
1 cup cooked amaranth
Tamari or shoyu to taste**

Amaranth is primarily used as a bread grain, but here it gives its special flavor to a refried grain dish. Change the first-stage cooking liquids for interest. It is your choice on how long to refry this dish; the longer the fire time, and the more oil, the crustier the grain; less of either will give a softer result. Both are desirable. I think of the crustier version as a winter dish, and the softer grains as a summer dish.

Yield: 2 servings

1. Heat a skillet over medium heat and add oil. Add garlic, green onion, zucchini, and red pepper one at a time and cook until they are sealed and soft.

2. Mix cooked amaranth gently into the vegetables. Cook 5 minutes.

3. Season to taste with tamari before serving. Use the zig-zag seasoning-without-measuring motion to determine how much tamari to use.

SERVING SUGGESTIONS: Serve hot. Amaranth and vegetables make a complete meal; accompany with a raw vegetable salad or relish.

Process

Pretreatment
NONE
First Stage
STEEP
Second Stage
REFRY

GRAIN: Prepare the amaranth in your favorite first-stage cooking method. Since this grain is bitter, I suggest a strong cooking liquid like garlic, ginger, or rosemary water or beer to offset it. Perhaps a teaspoon of rice syrup in the cooking liquid would help. Rice, buckwheat, millet, Job's tears, teff, quinoa, and oats would also work in this dish.
OIL: A light oil works well here. I used light sesame, but safflower oil or ghee would also be compatible. In summer you need only enough to coat the bottom of a skillet; in winter you may wish to use more.
SALT SEASONING: Replacing the tamari or shoyu with umeboshi vinegar, an alternative salt seasoning, adds a dimension of braising.
HERBS AND SPICES: I recommend strong herbs and spices such as cilantro, sage, rosemary, garlic, or ginger.

ALTERNATIVE
COOKING METHODS
Pretreatment
DRY-ROAST
First Stage
BAKE
BOIL

VEGETABLES: Frequently the refrying method uses major vegetables. Go with what is in season: in the cooler months, onions, carrots, cabbages, burdock, and winter squashes; in warm weather, zucchini, peppers, and other summer vegetables. Cut the vegetables in small, even shapes to cook evenly and thoroughly with the grain.

Refried Sweet Rice and Olive Patties

In this delectable and different variation on refrying, the grains are mixed with vegetables and pressed together into patties. You could make it by the conventional refrying method, sautéing the vegetables and dill for a minute, then adding the grain and seasoning.

Yield: 6 patties (2–3 servings)

1. Mix vegetables and dill into rice. Shape into burgerlike patties.

2. Heat skillet over medium to medium-high heat and add oil. Refry the patties, turning them when they are golden brown.

3. Season on each side with tamari or shoyu before serving.

SERVING SUGGESTIONS: Like other refried dishes, this doesn't need a sauce. Serve it with a bean soup or bean salad.

2 cups cooked sweet brown rice
½ cup sliced green onion
¼ cup diced red pepper
5 to 10 brine-cured olives, pitted and minced
1 tablespoon dry dill weed
3 tablespoons olive oil
3 tablespoons shoyu or tamari

Process

GRAIN: The glutinous nature of sweet rice makes it hold together beautifully in patties. But this is a great dish with any first-stage grain that holds together with a little pressing; try millet, rice, buckwheat, teff, or amaranth.

OIL: Olive oil is compatible with the olives that are mixed into the grain. Sesame oil with sesame seeds or hazelnut oil with hazelnuts would be alternative combinations.

SALT SEASONING: Olives contribute some salt. Tamari or shoyu balances the generous amount of oil that makes this dish yummy. Umeboshi vinegar would also be a delicious choice for the final touch.

HERBS AND SPICES: Dill weed is light in flavor. When used alone as it is in this dish, its contribution is subtle. Other herbs such as oregano or arugula would also be good, but stick to a single choice.

VEGETABLES: Olives, green onion, and red pepper are decorative vegetables. Parsley, cooked carrots, and cooked burdock root are alternatives for color and flavor.

Pretreatment
NONE
First Stage
PRESSURE-COOK
Second Stage
REFRY

ALTERNATIVE
COOKING METHOD
NONE

Fried Rice With Brussels Sprouts, Tarragon, and Mustard

1½ tablespoons dark sesame oil
½ cup diced onion
5 brussels sprouts, quartered
2 tablespoons fresh tarragon leaves
2 cups cooked rice
1 tablespoon umeboshi vinegar
1 teaspoon prepared mustard
¼ cup chopped chives

This gem of a dish was created by Pam Hagel during improvisation. Pam didn't feel like cooking that day; she said she just didn't have any ideas. So she started with a single ingredient, mustard. Umeboshi vinegar followed, and then she chose refrying as the cooking method. The grain on hand was pressure-cooked rice. The other ingredients followed naturally. The dish emerged as the perfect reflection of Pam's character. She is courageous and daring; this dish is full of bold flavors.

Yield: 2½ cups (4 servings)

1. Heat a skillet over medium heat and add oil. Cook onion until clear and add brussels sprouts, sealing them in oil. Add rice and cook covered or uncovered, stirring occasionally, until sprouts are bright green and almost fully cooked, about 5 minutes.

2. Combine umeboshi vinegar and mustard in a small bowl and add to rice. Cook uncovered for another 5 minutes.

3. Mix in chives and serve.

TECHNIQUE NOTE: Heat the skillet first to help you determine how much oil to use. Sauté the vegetables and herbs before you add the cooked grain. Cook uncovered if you want a little crust. Use the seasoning-without-measuring technique to apply the salt seasoning, zig-zagging across the skillet as many times as it is deep (see p. 16).

SERVING SUGGESTIONS: This dish, served with crushed sesame seeds and a light soup, will make a great breakfast, lunch, or dinner. Try Sesame Salt (p. 179) as a condiment.

Process

Pretreatment
NONE
First Stage
PRESSURE-COOK
Second Stage
REFRY

GRAIN: Pressure–cooked rice was on hand, but kasha, millet, quinoa, or Job's tears would also be good with the very same ingredients.
SALT SEASONING: Umeboshi vinegar provides both salty and sour taste. Shoyu, tamari, or diluted miso would also work in this dish.
OIL: The more oil you use in refrying, the crustier your dish will be. Needing a jolt of intense flavor, Pam chose dark sesame. Light sesame and olive would also be successful.

HERBS AND SPICES: I told Pam to go to the garden to sniff the herbs in order to make her choice. Choosing tarragon to accompany mustard (a traditional combination), she also picked some chives, which added a light touch to the otherwise strong flavors in this dish.

VEGETABLES: An onion is fundamental to refried rice; other members of the onion family also work beautifully (leek, green onion). I had never seen brussels sprouts in this traditional dish, but they are terrific. Make sure they are slightly soft, to take in the mustard and umeboshi flavorings.

ALTERNATIVE
COOKING METHODS
First Stage
STEEP
BAKE

Mexican-Style Refried Kasha

This basic second-stage method is extremely simple. Possibilities for variations are infinite. Keeping vegetables and cooked grain at hand helps me prepare speedy meals and keeps my food costs down.

2 cups cooked kasha
3 tablespoons olive oil
2 tablespoons garlic
1 teaspoon chili powder
2 teaspoons minced fresh
 oregano
¼ cup sliced green onions
¼ cup diced celery
¼ cup diced red pepper
1 tablespoon tamari

Yield: 3 servings

1. Heat skillet over medium heat. Add oil, herbs and spices, green onions, celery, and red pepper, sealing each in oil. Add kasha and sauté for 3 to 5 minutes. Season with tamari.

SERVING SUGGESTIONS: Serve warm or at room temperature with a light soup.

Process

GRAIN: Rice, millet, quinoa, and Job's tears would make fine alternatives. Prepare them in a simple first-stage method without vegetables.

SALT SEASONING: Tamari can be replaced with shoyu, diluted miso, or umeboshi vinegar.

OIL: Ghee makes a delicious substitute for olive oil; light sesame will also work in this dish.

HERBS AND SPICES: The combination here is Mexican in inspiration. You could change the entire character by using fresh grated ginger, garlic, and cilantro or arugula.

Pretreatment
DRY-ROAST
First Stage
STEEP
Second Stage
REFRY

ALTERNATIVE
COOKING METHOD
NONE

Marinating

Marinating is the easiest, most impressive, and potentially most creative cooking method for grain. Think of tabouli and other grain salads. The fun part is inventing marinades, adding spices and herbs, and changing cooking liquids. Dry individual grains soak up the flavoring better than sticky grain. Usually served chilled, marinated grain dishes can age in the refrigerator for a week, and the flavors become more integrated. The stronger you make the cold sauce, the more sitting time it takes to integrate the flavors and the longer the dish will keep. This is a great dish for people who take lunches to work, or who have little time to cook. As in braising, the liquid (cold sauce) controls the flavor of the dish. The chart on page 120 shows possibilities for mixing and matching a variety of oils, cooking liquids, and herbs and spices. The trickiest part of preparing a cold sauce for marinade is creating enough volume of cooking liquid so the grain can soak. Marinades for vegetables use more oil than a grain marinade will use, while grain marinades can handle more vinegar or such flavor than a vegetable marinade. This is explained in more detail in the sauces chapter.

PROCEDURE

- Cook grain, using any combination of first-stage cooking method and pretreatments that will create an individual, dry texture.
- You may cool the grain or put it into the marinade hot. When the grain is precooled, you will have a more accurate taste reading on the potency of the marinade. When the grain is hot, build extra strength into the marinade, because the moisture in the hot grain will dilute some of the potency.
- Add decorative vegetables, seeds, or nuts if desired, for color and added texture.
- Let the grain and marinade sit together for at least an hour if possible. Cover and refrigerate before serving.

"Let first the onion flourish there,
Rose among the roots, the maiden-fair
Wine scented and poetic soul
Of the capacious salad bowl"

Robert Louis Stevenson

MARINATING:
To soak cooked grain in a cold sauce.
ENERGETICS:
Like resting in a cool, moist place.
TEXTURE:
Crunchy or soft; saturated.
FLAVOR:
Mild or strong, sweet, pungent, spicy, or herbal, depending on marinade.
COMPATIBLE COOKING METHODS:
Dry-roast, sauté, and all first-stage cooking methods, although pressure-cooked grains could be too sticky.

Oats in Raspberry-Mint Marinade

Dry-roasting oats helps them open up to receive the marinade. It also makes this traditional "feed grain" tastefully appeal to our palate. Marinating is the perfect soothing follow-up to the turbulent boiling method.

Yield: 2 cups (4 servings)

Combine oil, salt, vinegar, mint, onion, and oats in a large bowl. Mix well and let sit at least 1 hour. Store in refrigerator.

SERVING SUGGESTIONS: This can be served at room temperature, but I like it best cold. A hearty soup will complete this meal.

4 tablespoons hazelnut oil
½ teaspoon sea salt
8 tablespoons raspberry vinegar
4 tablespoons fresh mint leaves, minced
½ cup thinly sliced red onion
2 cups cooked whole oats (dry-roasted and boiled)

Process

GRAIN: Only whole oats work in this dish; steel-cut or rolled oats will become too mushy. Millet, quinoa, and rice would be terrific options.

COOKING LIQUID: Use plain water for the first-stage boiling, perhaps flavored with a cinnamon stick. Other vinegars could substitute for raspberry vinegar in the marinade, but do try it with raspberry vinegar; it is delightful. The stronger the vinegar, the less you need to use.

OIL: There are so few ingredients in this dish we need to make each one count. Hazelnut oil matches raspberry vinegar in its delicacy. Of course, olive and sesame oil will fill the same function, but if you want a truly unique dish with simple, simple oat groats, invest in hazelnut oil.

HERBS AND SPICES: Fresh mint, and lots of it, is all that is needed here.

VEGETABLES: Red onions provide decoration as well as strong flavor. I have been modest in my measurement of onion in the recipe. I encourage you to add as much as you like, since this single item has a terrific effect on the whole dish.

Pretreatment
DRY-ROAST
First Stage
BOIL
Second Stage
MARINATE

ALTERNATIVE
COOKING METHODS
First Stage
STEEP
BAKE

Oat Groats in Sweet Carrot Marinade

2 teaspoons olive oil
½ onion, diced
1 clove fresh garlic, minced
2 medium carrots, diced
Juice of 2 oranges (about 1 cup)
1 teaspoon umeboshi paste
1½ tablespoons mirin
2 cups cooked whole oats (dry-roasted and boiled)
½ cup parsley
Tamari-toasted almonds, slivered, for garnish

This hot marinade created during improvisation class by Margaret Walker and Trish Gillis is a great example of the creative process. In twenty years a warm marinade never occurred to me. Boiling the oats keeps them individual in character, and dry-roasting enhances their flavor.

The carrots were cooked in a pressure cooker because it was the only pot available, but I loved the way it enhanced their natural sweetness. You could also prepare this marinade in any pot with a heavy lid.

Yield: 2 cups (4 servings)

Heat a pressure cooker over medium-high heat. Add oil and sauté onions, garlic, and carrots. Add orange juice and umeboshi paste and pressure-cook for 2 minutes. Cool pot and release pressure according to manufacturer's instructions. Add mirin and parsley and mix oats into the carrot marinade.

SERVING SUGGESTIONS: This is an unusual and delicious dish. Serve it warm if possible, not hot, or at room temperature. Garnish with slivers of roasted tamari almonds, or other nuts and seeds.

Process

Pretreatment
DRY-ROAST
First Stage
BOIL
Second Stage
MARINATE

ALTERNATIVE
COOKING METHODS
First Stage
BAKE
STEEP

GRAIN: Although I haven't tried them, my sense is that millet, quinoa, and rice would like this presentation also.
SALT SEASONING: Umeboshi paste becomes the salt seasoning in the marinade. It is light, and effective in balancing the sweet flavors of carrot, orange, and mirin.
OIL: Olive, light sesame, and hazelnut oils work equally well in this dish.
HERBS AND SPICES: There is just a hint of garlic in the recipe. I don't encourage too much more—subtlety counts here.

Warm Mediterranean Millet Marinade

This is one of my all-time favorite marinades. It is adapted from my father's famous vinaigrette salad dressing. I use this dish in my classes to illustrate the technique of marinating grain dishes and to inspire the students' creativity.

Yield: 6 servings

1. Combine lemon juice, vinegar, olive oil, garlic, sea salt, basil, and pepper. Blend in blender or mix vigorously by hand.

2. Toss cucumber and tomato in marinade, then add warm cooked millet. Mix well.

SERVING SUGGESTIONS: Serve at room temperature or warm with bean soup, pâté, or a side dish of vegetable protein.

2 tablespoons lemon juice
4 teaspoons balsamic vinegar
2 tablespoons olive oil
2 cloves garlic, minced
¼ teaspoon sea salt
3 tablespoons fresh basil
1 teaspoon black pepper
2 cups English cucumber, diced
1 cup cherry tomatoes
3 cups freshly cooked millet

Process

GRAIN: Any grain works in this cooking method. My least favorite is buckwheat.

COOKING LIQUID: For additional flavor, boil the millet in garlic or turmeric-flavored water. Strong vinegar and lemon combine to cut through the heaviness and moisture of warm grain. Play with the varieties at hand.

OIL: Olive oil helps the flavors to cover the grain. Light sesame or hazelnut would also be good.

SALT SEASONING: Sea salt pulls the flavors out of the individual ingredients. Vegetable salt and miso would also work.

HERBS AND SPICES: A traditional Mediterranean combination of fragrant herbs, basil and garlic, is essential in this simple marinade. Change the herbs by the sniff-and-taste test.

VEGETABLES: Cucumber and tomato are both decorative and major in this dish. If you choose other vegetables, balance their color, texture, and shape with the grain.

Pretreatment
DRY-ROAST
First Stage
BOIL
Second Stage
MARINATE

ALTERNATIVE
COOKING METHOD
NONE

Wild Rice Salad

2½ cups water
1 teaspoon mulling spices, tied in cheesecloth or in a tea ball
1 cup wild rice, dry-roasted
Pinch of sea salt
Juice of 1 orange
1 tablespoon mayonnaise
1 teaspoon horseradish
3 cloves garlic, minced
2 cups broccoli (florets and diced stems), blanched
⅛ cup slivered red onion
½ cup salted roasted cashews

A private client wanted a wild rice salad. I dry-roasted and steeped this hearty grain to open its tight skin. Then I stumbled over the mulling spices in the cupboard. Of course, they would balance the earthy flavors of wild rice and make it the focus of the salad. I was truly surprised by the magnificence of this dish.

Yield: 3 cups (6 servings)

1. Bring water, spices, and salt to a boil in a heavy-bottomed saucepan. Add rice, cover, reduce heat to medium, and steep until all the liquid is absorbed, about 60 minutes.

2. Combine orange juice, mayonnaise, horseradish, and fresh garlic in a large bowl. Mix with a fork and add broccoli, onions, wild rice, and cashews. Toss and mix well. Store in refrigerator.

SERVING SUGGESTIONS: Serve chilled or freshly made at room temperature.

Process

Pretreatment
DRY-ROAST
First Stage
STEEP
Second Stage
MARINATE

GRAIN: Prepare wild rice for the marinade by dry-roasting and steeping in water and mulling spices (cinnamon, cloves, and orange peel). Other kinds of rice such as royal, basmati, or long-grain brown and other grains such as millet, oats, quinoa, or Job's tears are also suitable for this dish.

COOKING LIQUID: Orange juice makes a sweet base for this strong-flavored grain. Mirin is an option if you need more volume.

SALT SEASONING: The only salt in this dish is from the salt on the roasted cashews. You could add miso or tamari to the liquid but try the suggestions of this dish once.

OIL: Mayonnaise is mostly oil. If you don't want to use a mayonnaise-style sauce, I suggest a clear marinade of sesame oil, rice vinegar or lemon juice, and miso or tamari. See Cold Sauces on pages 171–78 for other ideas.

HERBS AND SPICES: Fresh garlic and horseradish make this dish interesting. Fresh ginger juice (see p. 83) would be a possibility with or without the garlic.

ALTERNATIVE
COOKING METHODS
First Stage
BAKE
PRESSURE-COOK
BOIL

VEGETABLES: Broccoli can be brilliant when slightly cooked to its brightest green. Rinse in cold water to retain the color. Red onion complements the color scheme of this dish and adds a pungent flavor to the sweet marinade.

Teff Caviar Stuffing

Teff glistens like caviar. If you don't want to use this as a formal appetizer, cut up the olives and serve it as a salad.

Yield: 4–6 appetizer servings

1. Combine onion, red pepper, and cooked teff and mix in Herbal Marinade. Marinate for at least 1 hour. Stuff the teff mixture into olives.

⅛ cup green onion, minced
⅛ cup sweet red pepper, minced
¾ cup cooked teff
⅓ cup Herbal Marinade (p. 173)
20 large pitted olives (green, black, or a combination)

Process

GRAIN: This is a perfect use for teff because it is so small and it holds together. This dish would also work with amaranth.

COOKING LIQUID: Water is the simplest cooking liquid for the first stage, but you could use more flavorful liquids if they are compatible with the marinade (for example, garlic water with Mediterranean-style marinade, or ginger water with an Oriental-style marinade). Cooking liquids for the second stage (vinegar, lemon juice, mirin, wine) play the accent role in the composition.

OIL: Use a flavorful oil for the marinade. In this dish olive oil is most appropriate with the herbs and olives. If you decide to stuff radishes, peppers, or cucumbers, for example, you could use an Oriental-style marinade with dark sesame oil.

SALT SEASONING: Balance your salt seasoning with the flavors of the marinade. See the Traditional Flavor Combinations chart on page 25 for ideas.

VEGETABLES: Decorative vegetables stand out against the plain grain. Black olive, red pepper, or parsley, minced not too small, add dashes of color. Use the teff mixture to stuff a variety of vegetables such as olives, cucumbers, radishes, or peppers.

Pretreatment
DRY-ROAST
First Stage
BAKE
Second Stage
MARINATE

ALTERNATIVE
COOKING METHODS
Pretreatment
DRY-ROAST
First Stage
BOIL
STEEP
Second Stage
MARINATE

Quinoa Salad With Grapes and Roasted Cashews

2 tablespoons raspberry
   vinegar
1 tablespoon mirin
¼ teaspoon sea salt
2 teaspoons dill
1 celery rib, diagonally
   sliced
½ cup red seedless
   grapes, cut in half
2 cups cooked quinoa
⅓ cup tamari-roasted
   cashews

I wanted to make a quinoa salad that was quite different from the quinoa dishes in the salad bars and delis around Boulder. This dish surprised me in its complete originality and satisfying taste. It looks pretty too.

Yield: 4 servings

In a large bowl, combine all ingredients, mixing them in one at a time in order. Let sit 1 hour or more to allow the flavors to mingle.

SERVING SUGGESTIONS: Serve at room temperature or chilled, with a hearty vegetable soup and a bean dish.

Process

Pretreatment
NONE
First Stage
STEEP
Second Stage
MARINATE

GRAIN: Cooked quinoa responds to a marinade if it isn't too wet. Make sure you drain it well after washing so no extra water lingers in the first-stage method. Dry-roasting enhances the texture, but is not necessary.

COOKING LIQUID: Accent liquids such as raspberry vinegar and mirin send this dish into delightful culinary dimensions. Because of their strength of character, no extra volume is needed here; grapes add their own natural juice. Raspberry vinegar matches the light fruity character of this dish. Apple cider vinegar can be a substitute, but try it at least once with raspberry vinegar.

OIL: Cashew nuts provide the oil in this dish. Other nuts or seeds like pistachios, pecans, or sunflower seeds can also be roasted a bit and used in place of cashews (although I don't like the flavor of tamari on pecans).

SALT SEASONING: Vegetable salt or light miso could replace sea salt.

HERBS AND SPICES: Fresh or dried dill weed keeps a lightness in this dish. Alternative herbs could be fresh arugula, mint, or marjoram.

ALTERNATIVE
COOKING METHODS
Pretreatment
DRY-ROAST
First Stage
BAKE
BOIL

FRUITS AND VEGETABLES: Red grapes are among the decorative "vegetables" in this salad. Fresh fruit and grain rarely meet, but celery, with its watery content and characteristic crunch, harmonizes the two.

Marinated Buckwheat Groats
With Fennel and Beets

You really should try this even if you don't like beets. It is a variation on my favorite beet recipe. I usually like buckwheat only when it's been roasted first, but here I like it because it's with something I love.

Yield: 3-4 servings

1. In a medium mixing bowl, dissolve salt in vinegar and oil. Add cooked beets, fennel, and buckwheat groats, in that order.

2. Mix well and chill about 1 hour before serving.

TECHNIQUE NOTE: Mix the vegetables in the marinade first. This boosts their flavor and helps the salad in general, since grain is denser.

SERVING SUGGESTIONS: I prefer this chilled rather than at room temperature. Accompany it with a hearty soup.

¼ teaspoon sea salt
2 to 3 tablespoons apple cider vinegar
1 tablespoon olive oil
⅓ cup cooked beets
1 cup diced fresh fennel (bulb, stalk, and leaves)
1 cup cooked buckwheat groats (steeped)

Process

GRAIN: Unroasted buckwheat groats are a bit slippery and extremely bland. Other grains would also receive the dashing color and flavors of this dish well.

COOKING LIQUID: Other vinegars such as balsamic and raspberry could replace the cider vinegar. Sniff and taste.

OIL: Olive oil was chosen here, but hazelnut or light sesame would also be good.

HERBS AND SPICES: Fresh fennel performs as both herb and vegetable in this dish.

VEGETABLES: Cooked beets act as the major vegetable. Carrots and cucumbers would be good alternatives.

Pretreatment
NONE
First Stage
STEEP
Second Stage
MARINATE

ALTERNATIVE
COOKING METHOD
NONE

Amaranth and Fresh Corn in Cashew-Miso Marinade

2½ cups vegetable
  bouillon
1 ear fresh corn
¼ cup dry-roasted
  amaranth

MARINADE
1 teaspoon cashew butter
½ teaspoon light miso
1 tablespoon mirin
½ tablespoon rice vinegar
Orange or pineapple juice
  (optional)
1 teaspoon rice syrup
½ teaspoon fresh ginger
  juice
1 slivered green onion

This dish was created during the season of truly fresh corn on the cob. So to make use of the whole vegetable and strengthen the cooking liquid, I shaved off the kernels of corn from the cob and placed the naked cob into the vegetable bouillon. The cold sauce given here is only one of the possible variations for marinating these grains; try also Sweet and Sour Marinade (p. 174), Cold Avocado Sauce (p. 175), or the marinade in Warm Mediterranean Millet Marinade (p. 141).

Yield: 1 cup (2 servings)

1. Bring broth to a rapid boil. Cut corn kernels from cob and set aside. Add cob to broth and cook 5 minutes; remove. Add dry-roasted amaranth and boil 9 minutes, or until it has a unified texture inside and out.

2. Strain, reserving liquid for soup if you like the flavor. Add corn kernels to hot grain and cover, steaming the corn in the hot grain.

3. Optional: Rinse the grain in cool or tepid water and let drain completely before putting it in the marinade.

4. Blend marinade ingredients and add cooked grain.

Process

Pretreatment
DRY-ROAST
First Stage
BOIL
Second Stage
MARINATE

GRAIN: Dry-roasting this grain helps it become individual enough to receive the marinade. The boiling time will vary with altitude; after 9 minutes at 5,000 feet it was just right, a bit chewy. At sea level, 9 minutes may be just right or it might turn the grain soggy. So please, check the grain as it cooks. Individual grains will be a variety of textures when done. Try this marinade with quinoa, rice, millet, or oat groats.
COOKING LIQUID: To me, whole amaranth needs as much help as it can get. Whether you use a vegetable bouillon or a homemade vegetable stock, this grain likes vegetable flavors. The marinade uses mirin and rice vinegar, two especially compatible ingredients. If you are increasing the recipe to make more than two servings, you might wish to include another cooking liquid that will create volume, not

just accent. Orange juice or pineapple juice will induce a sweetness, lemon or lime a sour flavor. Since this grain is on the bitter side, I would go with the sweet flavor. You might like to add a teaspoon of rice syrup to this dish to buffer the bitterness.

SALT SEASONING: None is needed for the first stage if using salted bouillon; otherwise add a pinch of sea salt to the liquid. Choose a light miso or the salt seasoning in the marinade; I used light barley miso, but white, red, or yellow miso will do nicely. You might want to indulge by using a bit more of this not-too-salty salt seasoning.

OIL: Cashew butter provides the oil in this marinade. Almond and filbert butters would also be exceptionally good.

DECORATIVE VEGETABLES: For a simple dish, a small, slivered green onion will do. But anything goes in this style of cookery: parsley, cilantro (watch out, it's strong), red peppers, or whatever cooked vegetables you like. Try dry-roasted, tamari-flavored pumpkin or sunflower seeds or pine nuts as garnish.

ALTERNATIVE
COOKING METHODS
First Stage
STEEP
BAKE

Sauces

There is no way around the fact that grains are very plain, teetering on the edge of bland and boring. Simple grain can be embellished by playing with texture, vegetables, herbs, and spices. Sauces add excitement. Why serve first-stage grain dishes naked when satisfying sauces take little time and charge your creativity?

It's easy to prepare sauces that aren't dependent on animal and dairy foods. In this book hot sauces are defined by their binding agents (beans, vegetables, flour, nuts, or starch). Each hot sauce is composed of a binding agent, cooking liquid, and seasonings. Cold sauces are defined by how they are used — as marinade, dipping sauce, or topping. Both hot and cold vegetable sauces offer plenty of variety for the creative cook.

Consider three factors when making a sauce: flavor, strength, and substance. Flavor is derived from the choice of ingredients. Would a strong balsamic vinegar be good with hazelnut oil? Or is it better to use a light rice vinegar or fruity raspberry or apple cider vinegar? Strength is determined by the quantity and quality of ingredients. If a small amount of vinegar doesn't provide a strong enough flavor, add more. Fresh, good-quality ingredients offer strength; a dried-up old lemon probably won't have much strength. Substance (whether a sauce is thick or thin is easily adjusted) comes from the binding agents. If a sauce is too thin, add a binding agent, or reduce the liquid over heat. If a sauce is too thick, add some cooking liquid, integrate it with fire, and check the seasonings for strength.

Hot Sauces

There are five styles of hot vegetable sauces: flour, nut, vegetable, clear, and bean. Each has a distinct quality of substance. Usually I don't mix binding agents, but sometimes an occasion arises to combine two of them. For example, you may want to embellish a vegetable sauce with nut butter, or balance the richness of nut sauce with flour.

A hot sauce will thicken when it cools because the molecules are no longer being moved around by heat. Flour, bean, and starch sauces are bound in permanent suspension and will not separate after cooking; nut and vegetable sauces may separate.

Hot sauces taste much better *on* the food than off a tasting spoon or finger, so do your taste testing with the grain the sauce will go on. Salt seasonings are at the heart of a sauce; without them the sauce may refuse to integrate flavor or establish a healthy substance. You don't need a lot of salt seasoning, just enough to balance flavors.

HOT SAUCES

	BASE BINDING AGENT	COOKING LIQUID	OIL	SALT SEASONING
CLEAR	arrowroot kudzu cornstarch	stock water *wine *mirin vinegar juice	any oil or no oil	any *tamari
FLOUR	wheat pastry *rice quinoa barley oat corn	*stock *wine water	sesame corn safflower	sea salt
SEED/ NUT BUTTER or NUT MILK	peanut *cashew almond *filbert pistachio sesame seed	water stock *wine others in combination		*miso *umeboshi
BEAN	well-cooked beans	stock water beer vinegar lemon/lime juice	olive corn safflower	sea salt tamari
VEGETABLE	cooked roots flower vegetables vine vegetables onion	*stock water *wine	sesame olive corn safflower *hazelnut	vegetable salt sea salt umeboshi *light miso

Ingredients listed are only suggestions from the food categories. See the entire selection in the Foods to Have on Hand chart (pp. 12-16).

* = preferred selections

Flour Sauces

The English term for sauce is "gravy," from the French word for a kind of sauce made with flour or *grane* (grain). Between France and England a slip of the pen misspelled "grane" as "grave" and the name "gravy" stuck.

Between 1400 and 1600, the famous roux was born. No longer were stale bread and almond dust used as binding agents; instead, it was flour browned in fat. The sauce escapade was on. Today we enjoy myriad French-style sauces, and I get lost in all the names founded on French cities and provinces. What it boils down to is basic preparations (cooking methods) and ingredients.

In flour sauce, a mixture of flour and oil (roux) acts as a thickening agent. Traditional flour sauces include bechamel, white sauce, and brown sauce. Whole-wheat pastry flour is my most common choice, but rice, quinoa, rye, garbanzo bean, and corn flours also make good sauces. Whole-wheat pastry, rice, oat, and corn flour make smoother and lighter sauces than whole wheat, rice, and rye flours. Remember it's the amount of oil that makes the sauce smooth (the more, the smoother), and be aware of the flavor and color that will be created with your choice of flour. White sauce is prepared with clear cooking liquids; brown sauce is prepared with browned vegetables (if you don't use meat) and a brown roux. Bechamel sauce (named after its creator, Louis de Bechameil, a courtier of Louis XIV) is made from browned vegetables and milk, or, in our system, nut milk.

Flour sauces require a minimum of 20 minutes cooking time to integrate the seasonings, adjust the substance, and insure that the flour has been cooked. You can use a long method, which takes a little more time and imparts a richer flavor, or a quick method (see p. 152). Each has its own characteristics. The long method results in more grain flavor and a smoother texture; the quick method gives a milder grain flavor and a grainier texture. I use the quick method to adjust substance.

For a medium flour sauce use 2 tablespoons of oil, ⅓ cup of flour, and 1 cup of cooking liquid. The ratio of flour to oil can be anywhere from 1:1 to 3:1. Remember, oil is what makes this a sensual sauce; it carries the flavors of the grain and seasonings, binding them into a sauce of substance, flavor, and strength. Start with the ratio 1:1; you can reduce the oil next time if it is too rich.

PROCEDURE (LONG METHOD)

- Heat a heavy skillet or saucepan over medium heat and warm the oil or ghee.
- Add flour to the warm oil, stirring it carefully as it browns; about 1 to 2 minutes is enough to take the raw flavor out of the flour. Longer browning, 3 to 5 minutes, will give a richer flavor and a darker color, which will carry over to the sauce. (This mixture, called a roux, can be rolled after cooling into little balls, wrapped in wax paper, and stored in the freezer, ready for a quick sauce preparation.)
- Remove the skillet from the heat and let the roux cool down completely, or be ready for some fast stirring. Add cooking liquid to the saturated flour *very* slowly, blending it quickly with a whisk. A stream of liquid and constant stirring will prevent lumps if the cooking liquid is not too hot.
- Return the skillet to medium heat and add the salt seasonings, herbs, spices, and decorative vegetables. Cover and simmer for a minimum of 20 minutes (use a flame tamer), or until the flavors have blended and the grain does not taste raw.

PROCEDURE (QUICK METHOD)

The quick method is especially good for adjusting substance in any kind of sauce that may be too thin.

- Sauté the vegetables and herbs or spices in a generous amount of oil.
- In a separate bowl, combine the cool cooking liquid with flour and whisk together until well blended.
- Add this mixture to the vegetables and stir constantly with a whisk until the sauce has thickened.
- Adjust taste with salt seasonings and spices, cover, and cook for 20 minutes or longer until the flavors have integrated.
- Use a flame tamer for slow cooking and to prevent burning.

FLOUR SAUCE:
Sauce thickened with flour and oil (roux).
ENERGETICS:
A sauce of substance, graceful but strong.
TEXTURE:
Smooth or slightly grainy, depending on the kind of flour and the amount of oil used. Can be heavy or light.
FLAVOR:
A nutty flavor when dry-roasted or sautéed flour is used. Basic sauce is very plain and needs salt seasonings, herbs, and spices.
COMPATIBLE GRAIN DISHES:
Any hot grain dish.
FAVORITE USES:
Serve on Millet Mash, Party Rice, croquettes.

Rice Flour Sauce

This recipe uses the "slow" method of preparing flour sauce. The advantage of taking the time to do all the steps in the procedure is in the quality of the final outcome. Energetically, more time and care is given to this sauce and it shows.

Yield: 2½ cups (5–7 servings)

1. Heat skillet over medium heat and add oil and flour. Brown flour (only slightly if you want to keep the sauce white). Let the oil saturate the grains of flour.

2. Remove pan from heat. Very slowly add the water, whisking it into a corner of the flour until it has all been incorporated. Add the wine in the same way, whisking until all is smooth.

3. Add bay leaf, garlic, sea salt, red pepper, and white pepper. Cover and cook for 20 minutes or until flavors integrate.

4. Adjust seasonings and toss in parsley.

SERVING SUGGESTIONS: Party Rice, Millet Mash, or any first-stage cooked dish will like this sauce. In general, use when the dish you are serving it with contains vegetables.

4 tablespoons light sesame oil
8 tablespoons rice flour
2 cups water
½ cup dry white wine
1 bay leaf
2 cloves garlic
1 teaspoon sea salt
½ cup diced sweet red pepper
White pepper, to taste
2 tablespoons parsley, minced

Process

STYLE OF SAUCE: Flour sauce.

BINDING AGENT: Other flours, including those made of garbanzo beans, wheat, corn, rye, barley, quinoa, and Job's tears, are all suitable.

COOKING LIQUID: Water and wine could be replaced with vegetable stock or bouillon.

OIL: The kind of oil you use is not important. Consider the flavor of ghee, olive oil, and rich dark sesame oil. What is important is the way the herbs, spices, and salt seasonings go with the flavor of the oil.

SALT SEASONING: My preference is sea salt because there is a big job to do in integrating flavors of dull flour, thick oil, herbs and spices, and a variety of cooking liquids. Tamari, miso, or umeboshi are good to adjust the taste near the end of cooking if necessary.

HERBS AND SPICES: Garlic and bay leaf are almost standard for me when I make a flour sauce. Other spices (cumin, cardamom) and fresh herbs such as basil and dill are good also.

VEGETABLES: Decorative vegetables add flavor, but mostly they are needed to accent the creamy white sauce.

Curry Flour Sauce

2 tablespoons ghee
2 cloves garlic
½ cup diced green onion
⅛ cup diced sweet red
    pepper
4 tablespoons pastry
    wheat flour
½ cup dry white wine
1½ cups water
1 teaspoon vegetable salt
1 small bay leaf
½ teaspoon basil
2 teaspoons curry powder
White or black pepper
    (optional)

This recipe demonstrates the "quick" method for making flour sauce. It is a good technique for adjusting substance when a sauce is too thick. Mixing flour and water together before heating is a common approach to making gravy and thickening stews. When adjusting substance use only a little liquid, just enough to dilute the flour.

Yield: 2 cups (4–6 servings)

1. Heat a skillet over medium heat and add ghee. Sauté garlic, green onion, and red pepper.

2. Whisk flour with wine and water in a bowl. Pour flour mixture into the hot vegetables, whisking briskly and continuously to avoid lumps.

3. When flour and liquid has reached an even consistency, add vegetable salt, bay leaf, basil, curry powder, and black or white pepper.

4. Cover and cook for 20 minutes to integrate flavors. Remove bay leaf.

SERVING SUGGESTIONS: Great on any first-stage cooked grain.

Process

STYLE OF SAUCE: Flour sauce.
BINDING AGENT: Rice, quinoa, rye, corn, barley, and Job's tears flours are good substitutes.
COOKING LIQUID: Water and wine share the responsibility of creating both substance and flavor. Laurie conceived the idea of replacing water and wine with coconut milk. A good idea. Other nut milks are also possibilities, and would make this a combination sauce.
OIL: Ghee is a rich, smooth-tasting oil. Light sesame and olive oils are also good choices.
SALT SEASONINGS: Vegetable salt embellishes the base flavors more than simple sea salt. But sea salt will work fine and umeboshi is an option if it works with the wine flavors. Other salt seasonings are acceptable for flavor and function, but could change the color.
HERBS AND SPICES: Garlic, bay leaf, basil, and curry all work; be generous. Oil and flour soak up a lot of flavor.
VEGETABLES: Decorative vegetables are recommended. Red pepper and onion lend flavor, but they are chosen for color. Cut them small.

Nut Sauces

Prior to the 1400s, the common binding agent for sauces was bread soaked in ale or beef broth, followed by ground almonds called almond dust. Nut and seed sauces are incredibly luscious. In full flavor and creaminess they surpass other kinds of sauces. The strength of flavor from nuts and salt seasoning insures goodness with or without additional seasonings. Nuts and salt seasonings together expand in the cooking liquid, creating a smooth, rich substance.

Herbs and spices are not essential, but additional seasoning and cooking liquids do deepen the character and make the sauce more flavorful.

The binding agent can be fresh ground nuts or packaged nut butters. If you prepare your own nut butter or nut milk, you may choose to roast the nuts a bit first. Roasted nuts and dark salt seasonings will make a dark sauce, while raw nuts and light-colored salt seasonings will keep a sauce almost white. Start with nut butter or whole raw nuts. The ratio of nut butter to salt seasoning is approximately three parts nut butter to one part salt seasoning. The cooking liquid is usually water or wine.

When using prepared nut butter, use a whisk to blend the ingredients quickly. If you need to make nut butter or nut milk, use a blender or food processor. Nuts that are high in fat content can easily burn while cooking; use a flame tamer to moderate the heat after the mixture has thickened. A nice option with this special sauce is leaving little pieces of nut to provide an interesting texture.

PROCEDURE (HAND METHOD)

- Combine the nut butter and salt seasoning in a saucepan. Gradually add cool cooking liquid, stirring with a whisk until it looks like soup.
- Heat slowly, stirring until thick. Don't cover (it will overflow). Cook slowly for about 10 minutes; do not boil. This is a good place to use a flame tamer.
- When adding decorative vegetables and herbs or spices, cook long enough to allow the flavors to blend.

PROCEDURE (PROCESSOR METHOD)

Use this method if you are beginning this sauce with whole nuts instead of nut butter.

NUT OR SEED SAUCE:
A rich, creamy sauce created from nuts or seeds that have been ground to a paste and cooked with liquid and salt seasonings.

ENERGETICS:
Luscious and full of sensuality.

TEXTURE:
Smooth or crunchy, thick or thin.

FLAVOR:
Strong, rich.

COMPATIBLE GRAIN DISHES:
All dishes except refried and deep-fried (which already are rich in oil), and marinated (which has its own sauce).

FAVORITE USES:
Cashew with miso; almond and peanut with umeboshi as salt seasoning; sunflower butter with orange juice for cooking liquid.

- Chop nuts until they are very fine or they turn to paste.
- Add a small amount of the measured cooking liquid until the paste is wet. While the processor is going, add the remaining liquid. If you are not measuring, the consistency should look like soup.
- Add the salt seasonings, herbs, and spices.
- Heat the mixture slowly, stirring until thick. Cook for about 10 minutes. Do not boil.

Peanut Umeboshi Sauce

5 tablespoons peanut butter
2 tablespoons umeboshi vinegar
1 cup water
Lemon juice to taste (optional)

This recipe was my first great discovery that umeboshi works interchangeably with miso. I invented it during a private class, when the only nut butter and salt seasoning at hand were peanut butter and umeboshi paste. It is a delectable sauce if you like peanuts; their flavor will override the dish.

Yield: 1¼ cup (3–4 servings)

1. Blend peanut butter and umeboshi paste together and work in the liquid a little at a time. (Or put all ingredients in blender and blend.)

2. Cook in a saucepan over medium heat, stirring until mixture is thick and flavors have integrated, about 10 minutes. (Use a flame tamer to prevent burning.)

3. Add lemon juice to taste.

SERVING SUGGESTIONS: Serve on a grain cooked by any first-stage method. Party Rice, Sweet Rice With Teff, Baked Kasha, or Pressure-Cooked Job's Tears are a few possibilities.

Process

STYLE OF SAUCE: Nut butter.
BINDING AGENT: Peanut butter is the binding agent in this sauce. Cashew, almond, and filbert nut butters are also delicious.
COOKING LIQUID: Water for neutrality among the powerful companions.
SALT SEASONING: Umeboshi paste can be replaced by either light or dark miso.

Cashew Dill Sauce

This recipe is an example of combining herbs with an already complete sauce. I especially like this served with Baked Lemon-Dill Rice (p. 79).

Yield: 1 cup (3–4 servings)

1. Blend cashew butter and miso together and work in the water a little at a time. (Or put all ingredients in blender and blend.) Add wine.

2. Add dill and cook in a saucepan over medium heat, stirring until mixture is thick and flavors have integrated, about 10 minutes. (Use a flame tamer to prevent burning.)

3. Add lemon juice to taste.

SERVING SUGGESTIONS: Serve on a grain cooked by any first-stage method. Baked Lemon-Dill Rice, Sweet Rice Mochi, Party Rice, Sweet Rice With Teff, baked kasha, or Job's tears are a few possibilities.

5 tablespoons raw cashew butter
2 to 3 tablespoons white miso
¾ cup water
¼ cup dry white wine
4 tablespoons dill weed
Lemon juice to taste

Process

STYLE OF SAUCE: Nut sauce.

BINDING AGENT: You can use roasted cashew butter, but it is very deep in color and has extreme strength of flavor. Raw cashew butter keeps this sauce light in color, like a true creamy white sauce.

COOKING LIQUID: Water and wine share the position as cooking liquid. You can change the proportions, using equal water and wine or more wine than water, although the latter would be quite intense. Fruit juice is also an option, combined with water not wine.

SALT SEASONING: White miso was chosen to match the lightness of raw cashew butter. Other light misos such as red and yellow will also work. Tamari will turn the color too dark, and umeboshi vinegar is best used without wine.

HERBS AND SPICES: Dill weed, a light herb, matches the light quality of this sauce; even though there is a large dose of it for strength, the quality remains light. Oil and salt seasoning in this style of sauce swallow flavor, so be generous with herbs. Laurie made a great success of this sauce with basil replacing dill weed.

Creamy Almond or Hazelnut Butter Sauce

3 tablespoons hazelnut or
   almond butter
1½ tablespoons white
   miso
½ cup water

The first time you make this sauce, use water. The second time, use part wine. The third time, try fruit juice. See Sunflower Orange Sauce for ideas (p. 103).

Yield: ¾ cup (2 servings)

1. Blend nut butter and miso together and work in the liquid a little at a time. (Or put all ingredients in blender and blend.)

2. Cook in a saucepan over medium heat stirring until mixture is thick and flavors have integrated, about 10 minutes. (Use a flame tamer to prevent burning.)

SERVING SUGGESTIONS: Serve on grain cooked by any first-stage method. If the dish has vegetables within it, the sauce completes the dish nutritionally; if the grain is plain, add a vegetable dish to your meal.

Process

STYLE OF SAUCE: Nut sauce.
BINDING AGENT: Hazelnut or almond butter are equally delicious and interchangeable.
COOKING LIQUID: Water can be mixed with fruit juice for a special occasion. Use only enough liquid that when it is blended with the other ingredients the mixture will look like thin soup or milk. You can always thin the sauce after it has heated; it is more difficult to thicken it again.
SALT SEASONING: You can use any miso as long as you know that the darker it gets, the saltier it gets. Umeboshi paste and vinegar work well; tamari is not as delicious.
HERBS, SPICES, AND FLAVORINGS: Single herbs or minced orange zest can give a great variety to this basic sauce. Be sparing in the number of items you use; hazelnuts and white miso have a delicate, distinct taste of their own.

Clear Sauces

In the early twentieth century, Escoffier recognized that it was the starch that bound sauces, that it took many hours to cook flour sauces in order to activate their starch, and that then you still had to skim off the protein. Pure starch (arrowroot), already common in Oriental fare, was introduced into French sauce making as a time-saving ingredient; it replaced a grainy texture with a velvety one.

Available in natural food stores, arrowroot flour and kudzu root powder can create a very impressive sauce to support a grain dish—one that shines and shimmers. Bound by starch and liquid, a clear sauce can be used as a glaze when made thick and as a sauce when between thick and thin.

The binding agent has no color or flavor, but it guarantees a shine and velvety smooth substance. To get the most flavor out of this style of sauce, use a selection of potent vegetables that have been browned slowly for a long time (the oil you use here will be the only oil in the sauce); a strong, clear stock; salt seasonings; and/or herbs and spices. This noncommittal sauce provides a great chance to "tie it all together" when vegetables and seasonings are at loose ends.

Various starches, of which cornstarch is most common, will produce a clear sauce, but arrowroot and kudzu root are the natural choice. Unlike cornstarch, arrowroot and kudzu are not refined but carry the valuable energy of the whole. These starches are simply roots that are dried and ground to flour.

The following ratios are guidelines; you can add more or less than the suggested amounts as long as the starch is first mixed in cool liquid. If you need to thicken a clear sauce that has finished cooking, dilute a tablespoon or more of starch in a tablespoon of liquid. Add it slowly and stir constantly. If you want to thin the sauce, simply add cooking liquid until you reach the desired consistency.

One tablespoon of one or a combination of starches (kudzu and arrowroot) and 1 cup liquid creates a thin sauce for two servings. For a thick sauce, mix 1½ tablespoons starch with ⅔ cup liquid. A thick sauce becomes clear after it thickens; a thin sauce becomes clear before it thickens.

CLEAR SAUCE:
A shiny thick or thin sauce
that is transparent and
flavored by seasoning agents
and vegetables.
ENERGETICS:
Soothing and unobtrusive.
TEXTURE:
Smooth, glistening.
FLAVOR:
Totally dependent on
vegetables and seasonings.
COMPATIBLE GRAIN
DISHES:
All hot grain dishes except
oats.
FAVORITES:
Mushroom-Onion Sauce over
kasha; Sweet and Sour Sauce
with Rice Croquettes.

**2 tablespoons apple cider
vinegar**
3 tablespoons water
1 tablespoon mirin or sake
1 tablespoon white miso
**½ teaspoon arrowroot
starch**
3 leaves cilantro, minced
**1 teaspoon red pepper,
minced**

PROCEDURE

- Sauté vegetables, herbs, and spices until vegetables are almost completely cooked.
- In a measuring cup, blend the starch into the cold cooking liquids.
- Over medium heat, stir the liquid into the vegetables; stir constantly to avoid lumping. When the sauce has changed from cloudy to clear, it is ready. This only takes a few minutes.

Mock Mustard Clear Sauce

The inspiration for this oil-free sauce came from the idea of turning a braising liquid into a clear sauce. Shelly called it Mock Mustard for its similarities to the taste of mustard.

Yield: ¼ cup (2 servings)

1. Combine all ingredients in a saucepan.

2. Cook over medium heat, stirring until sauce becomes thick.

SERVING SUGGESTIONS: Serve with grain dishes that require oil, such as croquettes.

Process

STYLE OF SAUCE: Clear.
BINDING AGENT: Arrowroot starch.
COOKING LIQUID: Water and mirin.
SALT SEASONING: Miso acts as salt seasoning but leaves a cloudy clear sauce. Tamari would also be good.
HERBS AND SPICES: Cilantro could be replaced by parsley. Additional flavors could come from fresh ginger juice (see p. 83), onion juice, or grated onion.
VEGETABLES: Sweet red pepper is a decorative vegetable. Green onion or parsley would be alternatives or additions.

Mushroom-Onion Sauce

This sauce was inspired by my eating experience at Ratner's Delicatessen in New York City. It was a cold winter day and we walked a couple miles to this restaurant one Sunday morning. We were warmed by a generous serving of kasha smothered with a mushroom-onion sauce. Looking back fifteen years, I think their sauce included a bit of flour base.

Yield: 2 cups (4–6 servings)

3 tablespoons sesame oil
2 cups thinly sliced
   mushrooms
2 cups thinly sliced onions
1½ cups cold water
1½ tablespoons arrowroot
   starch
2 tablespoons tamari or
   shoyu

1. Heat a skillet over high heat and add oil. Sauté mushrooms until they squeak and are golden brown.

2. Add onions and sauté until they also are rich brown.

3. Mix cold water with arrowroot in a separate bowl and stir into the vegetables; cook, stirring until thick and translucent.

4. Add tamari to taste.

TECHNIQUE NOTE: Sautéing the vegetables to the point of dryness is essential. When they seem to be just above burning, add a pinch of salt. This draws their essence out into the pan. Capture these flavors with the solution of arrowroot and cooking liquid.

SERVING SUGGESTIONS: Serve this dish with kasha, rice, millet, or quinoa. Oats, Job's tears, teff, and amaranth are too slippery to receive this slippery sauce.

Process

STYLE OF SAUCE: Clear.

BINDING AGENT: Arrowroot starch.

COOKING LIQUID: Liquids other than water or in addition to water would change this dish considerably. Try mirin, rice vinegar, or wine. Flavors from the vegetables influence the cooking liquid as they become one in the broth.

OIL: Light or dark sesame oil, olive oil, or ghee all make mushrooms and onions taste delicious.

SALT SEASONINGS: Tamari or shoyu is the perfect choice for this caramel-colored sauce.

VEGETABLES: Vegetables are frequently the major ingredient in a clear sauce. Their flavors are a dominant factor, and they need to be cooked to a point of dryness. Cut them fairly small.

Sweet and Sour Clear Sauce

⅓ cup pineapple juice
⅓ cup apple juice
1½ tablespoons arrowroot
   starch
5 whole cloves
10 cardamom pods
1 tablespoon rice syrup
¼ teaspoon sea salt
1 tablespoon apple cider
   vinegar

This sauce is tangy and thick. By adding a lot of fruit chunks, you can make it into a chutneylike condiment to serve on a grain dish – preferably a dish with few vegetables, as fruit and vegetables are not always the best combination.

Yield: ½ cup (2–4 servings)

1. Combine pineapple and apple juice, arrowroot, cloves, cardamom, rice syrup, and sea salt in a saucepan. Mix well, diluting the starch in the liquids.

2. Bring to a slow boil, stirring constantly and cooking until mixture is thick and clear, about 2 to 3 minutes. Remove spices.

3. Add cider vinegar to taste.

SERVING SUGGESTIONS: Serve on colorful millet, quinoa, or rice. In general, use with a dry grain or one that has been dry-roasted.

Process

STYLE OF SAUCE: This variation of clear sauce depends on the flavors of the cooking liquid.
BINDING AGENT: Arrowroot flour can be replaced by kudzu or cornstarch. (Although cornstarch is not recommended in natural cookery.)
COOKING LIQUID: Pineapple juice, apple juice, and apple cider vinegar are the base flavors for this sauce. No need for sugar; these juices are very sweet.
SALT SEASONING: Sea salt helps to integrate the sweet and sour flavors. Umeboshi and tamari could be substituted.
HERBS AND SPICES: Sweet spices—clove and cardamom—are chosen to embellish the naturally sweet taste. Hot flavors from cilantro, arugula, cayenne, and garlic would add a great dimension.
FRUITS OR VEGETABLES: Consider the possibilities of adding pieces of fruit such as pineapple, raisins, or apricots.

Cauliflower and Wine Sauce

Created during improvisation by Rayma Skeen and Cameron Hollister, this sauce has a sophisticated character. The most common version of this sauce is seen in every Chinese restaurant and is known in some circles as "stir-fry." But don't confuse it with the technique for stir-frying vegetables, because that technique is slightly different.

Yield: 2 cups (3–4 servings)

1. Heat a skillet over high heat and add oil, garlic, leeks, cauliflower, celery, and fennel seeds. Sauté until dry and browned.

2. Lower heat to medium-low, add salt, and cook for 10 minutes, creating a slight caramelization with the vegetables. A cover is optional.

3. Mix wine, water, starch, and miso together, diluting the starch and miso in the liquid. Add the mixture to the vegetables and stir continuously while cooking the sauce about 3 to 5 minutes until it is almost clear. (Miso prevents this sauce from becoming completely clear.)

SERVING SUGGESTIONS: Any first-stage grain dish except oats would love this sauce.

1 tablespoon light sesame oil
2 cloves minced garlic
¾ cup sliced leeks
1 cup cauliflower, broken into small florets
½ cup celery, cut small
1 teaspoon crushed fennel seeds
1 teaspoon sea salt
¾ cup dry white wine
¾ cup water
1 tablespoon arrowroot starch
1 tablespoon light miso

Process

STYLE OF SAUCE: Clear.
BINDING AGENT: Arrowroot and/or kudzu.
COOKING LIQUID: Equal parts water and wine makes this a strong-flavored liquid.
OIL: Light or dark sesame, olive, and hazelnut oils are all good options for this sauce.
SALT SEASONING: Sea salt is essential; miso is not. Without sea salt the flavors have difficulty coming through.
HERBS AND SPICES: Cilantro, tarragon, or rosemary could each replace fennel.
VEGETABLES: Major vegetables are the source of flavor and interest for this sauce. The color is off-white. Specks of carrot, squash, or red pepper could be cooked in for decoration. Choose a variety of vegetables; use what is at hand.

Bean Sauces

Bean sauces rely on cooked beans as the binding agent. Bean cookery is an art in itself. The crucial part of making a successful bean sauce is to begin with a bean that has integrity — that is, a bean that leaves no trace of being hard and is not jumping out of its skin, but is velvety soft within a fine unbroken skin. Soaking and/or preboiling will help achieve this texture, but the most successful treatments for cooking beans are the following: Don't use any salt, salt seasoning, or packaged foods (such as canned tomatoes) until the beans are soft. Cook salt seasoning into beans for at least 10 minutes; this helps bring out their sweetness. Pressure-cooking is a guaranteed method for cooking beans with integrity and can save hours of pot watching. Kombu (a natural MSG) helps break down the proteins to make beans more digestible; use a 2-inch to 3-inch piece for 2 cups of beans.

Black turtle, red, garbanzo, and pinto beans are some favorite choices for bean sauces. Strong herbs and spices, sea salt, or other salt seasonings complete the flavors of this simple binding agent. A touch of oil is optional. How thick or thin you make the sauce will depend on the integrity of the bean when you begin. A thin bean sauce is suitable on light-weight grains such as buckwheat and quinoa. A thicker sauce is more appealing on sturdy grains like rice, Job's tears, oats, and millet.

PROCEDURE

- Blend the cooked beans with the bean broth in a food processor or blender.
- Sauté the herbs, spices, and decorative vegetables. Add the blended beans to the skillet with the seasonings.
- Adjust the thickness by adding cooking liquids. Remember that beans will thicken with further cooking.

BEAN SAUCE:
A smooth, velvety sauce created with well-cooked beans as the binding agent.
ENERGETICS:
Hearty and heavy.
TEXTURE:
Velvety smooth, thick or thin.
FLAVOR:
Depends on the choice of bean and spices; full flavor.
COMPATIBLE GRAIN DISHES:
All except marinated.
FAVORITES:
Black Bean Sauce on millet croquettes; red bean sauce on refried or plain rice or quinoa.

Black Bean Sauce

Bean sauce is a great way to make use of a pot of beans or bean soup. The beans *must* be soft before you blend them.

Yield: 2 cups sauce (6 servings)

1. In a blender, blend the beans with water to a smooth purée.

2. Heat a skillet or saucepan over medium heat and add oil. Sauté garlic, cilantro, and red pepper.

3. Add bean purée to herbs and pepper. Sprinkle salt over beans and cook for 10 minutes. Season to taste with tamari.

4. Adjust the substance by adding more cooking liquid if too thick or by cooking uncovered if too thin.

SERVING SUGGESTIONS: Best served over simple grain dishes: pressure-cooked rice, millet, or Job's tears. I especially like bean sauce over refried corn bread.

1½ cups soft-cooked black beans
⅓ cup water
1 tablespoon olive oil
2 tablespoons minced garlic
¼ cup minced cilantro
¼ cup diced sweet red pepper
Pinch of sea salt
1 tablespoon tamari to taste

Process

STYLE OF HOT SAUCE: Bean.

BINDING AGENT: Black beans are used in this recipe, but small red kidney, pinto, white, navy, or garbanzo beans or red lentils are also options for this basic style of sauce.

COOKING LIQUID: Water is simple, but if you have beer around, use beer in the bean sauce for a special dimension.

OIL: Oil is optional. I like to use it if the grain dish doesn't have any oil in it because the sauce will be twice as smooth and luscious.

SALT SEASONING: Salt needs to be cooked into the bean purée to help integrate the flavors of herbs, spices, and beans with the volume and flavor of the cooking liquid. Adjust the salt seasoning with tamari. The amount depends on how much oil is used in the sauce.

HERBS AND SPICES: Garlic is the spice; cilantro the herb. Change these around, using strong flavors when beans are dense and lighter flavors when beans are light. White beans with dill and red beans with chili powder are suggestions.

VEGETABLES: Decorative vegetables give this sauce something to talk about. Try sweet red pepper, parsley, cooked carrot.

Spicy Tofu Sauce

2 cloves garlic
1 small serrano chili
⅛ cup olive oil
½ cup tofu
⅛ cup white wine vinegar
1 tablespoon dried basil
½ teaspoon vegetable salt
1 tablespoon ginger juice
(see p. 83)
⅛ cup water

I like to blend the spices and oil together before other ingredients are added. This ensures the flavors will blend evenly and thoroughly. Remember, oil is the vehicle for flavor to travel in and about the other ingredients.

Yield: ⅔ cup (2 servings)

1. In blender or food processor chop garlic and chili; mix in oil until flavors blend.

2. Press the extra liquid from tofu and blend into the spiced oil. Add vinegar, basil, salt, and ginger juice. Blend well.

3. Adjust substance by adding water slowly to reach desired thickness.

HOT SAUCE: Warm in saucepan over medium-low heat for 5 minutes or until flavors blend.

COLD SAUCE: Cover and rest in refrigerator for one hour, or until flavors integrate.

SERVING SUGGESTIONS: Serve hot or cold over any first-stage cooked grain.

Process

STYLE OF SAUCE: Bean.
BINDING AGENT: Tofu (soybeans).
COOKING LIQUID: White wine vinegar for accent; water for substance.
SALT SEASONING: Vegetable salt adds flavor as well as function of salt. Other seasonings could also work.
OIL: Olive oil makes the texture smooth and rich. The only other oil I would choose would be hazelnut oil, but to use it I would also change the herbs and spices.
HERBS AND SPICES: These hot spices and herbs work well together. Other possibilities are fennel, arugula, or marjoram, especially when using hazelnut oil.

Vegetable Sauces

Most familiar sauces were developed within the French and Italian cuisines. The French were largely responsible for seductive sauces based on animal and dairy fats; the Italians relied on vegetable purées, originally vegetables like mushrooms and truffles, later tomatoes and basil.

Vegetables become binding agents when they are cooked soft and puréed. The substance of this purée depends on the kind of vegetables used and their strength of character, fiber, and water content. Root, flower, and vine-growing vegetables make excellent binding agents. Root vegetables like carrots, potatoes, parsnips, and beets grow beneath the ground. Vine family members like winter and summer squash crawl along the ground. Flower vegetables like cauliflower, broccoli, brussels sprouts, and cabbage bloom. Fruit vegetables like tomatoes, eggplant, okra, avocado, and peas hang at the end of plants. We can choose the energetics of a vegetable sauce by selecting the growing style (energy) of the vegetables.

The first style of vegetable sauce is simply a purée of vegetables, with the option of a small amount of another binding agent, such as flour or nut butter. The oil comes from sautéing the vegetables before cooking them to a very soft texture. The second style of vegetable sauce, which I call Vegetable Velvet Sauce, is incredibly sensual. Crispy fried vegetables are intentionally made soft, then blended into a sauce. The oil source and additional binding agent (flour) cook with the raw vegetables in the deep-fry method (vegetable tempura), then these crispy delights are cooked together in a broth. The vegetables soften and the crispy flour coating becomes soggy, perfect for blending into a rich-textured sauce.

PROCEDURE (STYLE #1)

- Cut vegetables into medium to large pieces.
- Heat oil in a saucepan or pressure cooker. Sauté the herbs, spices, and onion family first, then the main vegetables.
- Add a pinch of sea salt and only enough cooking liquid to cover ⅓ of the volume of vegetables.
- Cover and simmer or pressure-cook until very soft. Purée the vegetables with their cooking liquid. Add a tablespoon of nut butter if you want an extra creamy sauce.

VEGETABLE SAUCE:
VEGETABLE SAUCE:
A sauce from vegetables of
the root, vine, flower, or fruit
families cooked until soft and
blended to create substance.

ENERGETICS:
Sturdy, nourishing.

TEXTURE:
Slightly thick, but light and
moist.

FLAVOR:
Reflects that of the vegetables
and seasonings.

**COMPATIBLE GRAIN
DISHES:**
All except marinated.

FAVORITES:
Vegetable Sauce #1 with
baked quinoa; Vegetable
Velvet Sauce with pressure
cooked rice.

- Add salt seasonings and any decorative vegetables. Cook these together until the flavors become one.
- If an additional thickener is needed, use a small amount of another binding agent. If you choose flour or starch, the temperature of flour and liquid must match. The quick method for flour sauces works well for adding thickness. Use only a little cooking liquid to dilute the binding agent before it goes into the vegetable sauce.

PROCEDURE (STYLE #2 VEGETABLE VELVET SAUCE)

- Slice the vegetables into thin pieces.
- Mix equal parts flour and cold water together, just enough to form a thin batter.
- Dip the vegetable in the batter and then deep-fry (see p. 128).
- Place the fried vegetables in a dry pot and add cooking liquid up to ⅓ the volume of the vegetables. Season with salt seasonings, herbs, and spices.
- Bring to a slow boil and simmer until flour falls away from the vegetables and they are soft enough to blend into a sauce. Allow 30 minutes for the flavors to come together.

Squash, Rutabaga, and Onion Sauce

Yield: 5 cups (6–8 servings)

1. Heat a heavy-bottomed soup pot or pressure cooker and add oil. Sauté onion, leeks, squash, and rutabaga, sealing them one at a time.

2. Add salt and nutmeg and cook for 1 minute. Add water, cover, and simmer for 15 minutes or seal the pressure cooker, bring up to pressure, and cook for 5 minutes.

3. Blend the soft vegetables in a blender or food processor. Toss in parsley and serve hot.

SERVING SUGGESTIONS: This sweet, hearty sauce is delicious with fresh-cooked grain in any first-stage method, but I am partial to it with pressure-cooked short-grain brown rice.

3 tablespoons hazelnut oil
1 small onion, coarsely cut
1 cup sliced leeks, white part only
2 cups butternut squash, coarsely cut
1 medium rutabaga
½ teaspoon sea salt
½ teaspoon nutmeg (optional)
1 cup water
¼ cup parsley

Process

STYLE OF SAUCE: Vegetable #1.

BINDING AGENT: Leeks, onion, butternut squash, and rutabaga give a beautiful golden color. Cauliflower, carrots, and celery are also possibilities.

COOKING LIQUID: Stock or wine would be good additions or replacements for water.

OIL: Hazelnut oil is exceptional anytime. Olive and light sesame oils are also good options; dark sesame oil can make a strong-flavored sauce.

HERBS AND SPICES: Nutmeg was a whim in this dish. It is compatible with the sweet flavors of onion and squash, and balances the bitter taste of rutabaga. When cauliflower replaces squash and rutabaga, use basil, garlic, and tarragon.

VEGETABLES: This sauce wouldn't exist without major vegetables. They are the binding agent described above. Parsley as a decorative vegetable works well against the bright orange sauce. Red pepper is a great accent of color against white (cauliflower) or any other color.

Vegetable Velvet Sauce

¾ cup flour
¾ cup icy cold water
Safflower oil for frying
3 small zucchini, cut into
    medium pieces
2 medium carrots, cut into
    medium pieces
1 medium onion, cut into
    medium pieces
2 cups water
3 inches kombu
½ teaspoon vegetable salt
3 tablespoons tamari, or
    to taste

This luscious, rich, purely vegetable sauce may appear to be "a long run for a short slide" as my friend Bill Sanford calls a dish that takes extra steps to get to a seemingly simple end. Indeed it does take time to deep-fry vegetables, but you could use leftover vegetable tempura. I know you will like this special sauce.

Yield: 4 cups (6–8 servings)

1. Mix flour and water in a medium bowl.

2. Heat oil for deep-frying. Dip vegetables in flour and water mixture and cook in hot oil until crisp. Turn on both sides. Remove, drain on paper towels, and place in a dry saucepan.

3. Combine water, kombu, and salt with vegetables. Cover and steep for 7 minutes.

4. When vegetables are soft, blend in a blender. Add tamari to taste.

SERVING SUGGESTIONS: Serve hot over any first-stage cooked grain.

Process

STYLE OF SAUCE: Hot Vegetable #2.
BINDING AGENT: Flour, oil, carrots, onions, and zucchini compose this sauce. Other vegetables, like celery, winter squash, burdock, daikon, parsnips, rutabaga, cauliflower, leeks, and mushrooms are other possibilities. Mix a combination of flours for a more interesting sauce. Corn, rice, and arrowroot flours make a good wheat-free, tasty sauce.
COOKING LIQUID: Water is very plain, making the binding agents do all the work in producing flavor. A touch of wine, ginger juice, or vinegar could help add dimension and cut through the oil if you find this sauce too bland.
SALT SEASONING: Vegetable salt helps the vegetables cook and tamari does the final seasoning to taste. Miso and umeboshi would be possible alternatives, but taste them with the combination of vegetables you are using before indulging in one or the other.

Cold Sauces

Cold sauce is a category that includes marinades, dipping sauces, and toppings from many cultures. Think of French vinaigrette (wine vinegar, fresh herbs, and olive oil) or its Mediterranean counterparts made with lemon juice in place of vinegar; the vegetable-based salsas of Latin America made with lime and hot chilies; the Oriental marinades and dipping sauces with their distinctive flavors of sesame or shoyu.

In grain cookery, cold sauces become marinades for grain salads or dipping sauces for crusty croquettes, and occasionally a mayonnaise-style topping.

Marinating, a second-stage method, relies on soaking cooked grain (preferably grain that is open and somewhat dry) in a combination of flavorful cooking liquids. Marinades can be sweet, pungent, herbal, or spicy.

Dipping Sauces are defined as thin, oil-free, salty, sweet, and/or sour liquids. They balance the oil in refried or deep-fried grains and act as condiments for finger foods, croquettes, millet sticks, and rice rolls.

Mayonnaise-style sauces are defined as thick cream sauces based on protein and oil. Tofu replaces egg as base for vegetable-style mayonnaise. Vegetables heavy in natural oil, such as avocados and olives, also become a base for thick sauces.

PROCEDURE

- Blend oil with herbs and spices.
- Add cooking liquids to establish substance.
- Mix in salt seasoning and adjust taste. Remember the taste should be very sharp. Grain will absorb the flavors.

"According to the Spanish proverb, four persons are wanted to make a good salad dressing: a spendthrift for oil, a miser for vinegar, a counsellor for salt, and a madman to stir it all up."

Abraham Hayward, 1801-1884, cited in *A Commonplace Book of Cookery* Robert Grabhorn

COLD SAUCES

OIL	LIQUID	SALT SEASONING	HERBS & SPICES
Avocado	Juice:	Sea salt	Herbs:
Sesame	Vegetable	Miso	Dill
Peanut	Sauerkraut	Tamari Shoyu	Basil
Olive	Apple	Umeboshi:	Tarragon
Safflower	Pineapple	Whole	Parsley
Walnut	Orange	Paste	Thyme
Dark sesame	Lemon	Vinegar	Marjoram
Olives	Vinegars:	Vegetable salt	Oregano
Nut butter:	Apple cider		Sage
Peanut	Rice		Rosemary
Almond	Umeboshi		Chives
Cashew	Wine		Bay leaf
Filbert	Malt		Spices:
Sesame-tahini	Water:		Pepper
	Plain		Coriander
	Rose	MISCELLANEOUS	Ginger
	Orange	Rice syrup	Garlic
	Nut milk	Barley malt	Nutmeg
	Mirin	Mustard	

STEPS FOR CREATING COLD SAUCES

1. Select one ingredient from each of these categories. If you are using a salt seasoning as a liquid, be careful not to oversalt. More than one ingredient from a single category may also work. Consult your taste buds and make enough liquid volume to dress your grain.

2. Blend these together in the following proportions:

    oil : vinegar : liquid

      1 : 1 to 2 : 5

Herbal Marinade

As a rule, allow one part (by volume) marinade to ten parts cooked grain. More liquid (2:10 or 3:10) is all right, but less may not be enough.

Yield: ⅓ cup (for 3–4 cups cooked grain)

Blend all ingredients in blender. Or make by hand: Crush garlic against the sides of a wooden bowl with a fork; add oil and crush the garlic into the oil. With vigor mix in basil, pepper, paprika, vinegar, and salt.

TECHNIQUE NOTE: Instead of using crushed garlic, consider using garlic water. To make this flavored liquid, put a little water in a bowl and press the garlic into it. This works particularly well if you want to remove the pieces of garlic from the salad. Garlic water permeates a marinade gracefully, and is easy to make.

SERVING SUGGESTIONS: Quinoa, Job's tears, teff, millet, oats, buckwheat, and rice all enjoy this basic marinade after they have been dry-roasted and steeped or boiled. To make a complete dish, use decorator vegetables. See recipes for marinated grain dishes on pages 138–47.

3 cloves fresh garlic
2 tablespoons extra virgin olive oil
6 tablespoons chopped fresh basil leaves
¼ teaspoon fresh ground pepper
1 teaspoon paprika (optional)
⅓ cup balsamic vinegar
½ teaspoon sea salt

Process

STYLE OF SAUCE: Marinade.

BINDING AGENT: Olive oil is usually my first choice for an herbal marinade, but other full-flavored oils, like hazelnut and dark sesame, can make a great contribution to a dish. Oil is optional in marinades but sometimes it rounds out the taste and carries the flavors of other ingredients. Only a small amount of oil is necessary; even if you need to double other ingredients, don't increase the amount of oil.

COOKING LIQUID: Among the selection of possible cooking liquids (see ingredient chart, pp. 12–13) balsamic vinegar is one of the strongest. Grain salads require more vinegar than vegetable salads, especially when hot grain is mixed in the marinade. Be aware, liquids may color your dish.

SALT SEASONING: Some salt is needed to help the flavors integrate. Plain sea salt is usually my choice, but I have had umeboshi and miso as divine-tasting seasonings in a marinade.

HERBS AND SPICES: Go wild! Use the taste-and-sniff test to determine compatible flavors, or use the chart of traditional combinations (p. 25) and play mix and match. Herbs add distinction and spices offer accent; again, don't use too many. I rarely use more than three herbs and spices together; simple is best.

Sweet and Sour Marinade

1 to 2 cloves minced
   garlic
1 tablespoon hazelnut oil
½ teaspoon sea salt
⅓ cup pineapple juice
⅓ cup rice vinegar
1 tablespoon rice syrup
1 tablespoon fresh
   oregano
White pepper to taste

Yield: ⅔ cup (for 3 cups cooked grain)

1. Blend all ingredients together.

SERVING SUGGESTIONS: I have enjoyed this sauce on cooked noodles and dry-roasted and steeped long-grain brown rice. I trust it with any dry, individually cooked grain.

Process

STYLE OF SAUCE: Marinade.
BINDING AGENT: Hazelnut oil is used to balance the cutting flavors of the cooking liquids. Dark sesame oil would also be delicious.
COOKING LIQUID: Pineapple juice and rice vinegar contribute both liquid volume and sweet and sour accent flavors.
SALT SEASONING: Sea salt brings the contrasting flavors together. Light miso or tamari would be great options.
HERBS AND SPICES: Garlic, oregano, and white pepper add dimension to the sweet and sour marinade. Other choices are cilantro or cinnamon.

Dipping Sauces

EASY DIPPING SAUCE
Yield: 2 servings
1 tablespoon tamari or
   shoyu
1 teaspoon mirin
1 teaspoon rice vinegar
Dash ginger juice to taste
   (see p. 83)

**EXTRA EASY DIPPING
  SAUCE**
Yield: 2 servings
1 tablespoon tamari
½ tablespoon rice vinegar
   or lemon juice

DAIKON DIPPING SAUCE
Yield: 2 servings
¼ cup grated daikon
1 tablespoon umeboshi
   vinegar
½ tablespoon lemon juice
1 tablespoon cilantro,
   minced

Dipping sauces are thin, salty, pungent, and oil-free. Use them primarily for balancing oil from refrying and deep-frying. Here are three samples of what a dipping sauce can be; put them together by mixing the ingredients in a small bowl.

Process

STYLE OF SAUCE: Dipping.
SALT SEASONING: Tamari, miso, or umeboshi.
COOKING LIQUID: Water, rice vinegar, mirin, or lemon juice.
HERBS AND SPICES: Garlic, mustard, ginger, cilantro, horseradish.
VEGETABLES: Daikon, green onion.

Topping-Style Sauces

Both mayonnaise-style and mashed-vegetable sauces act more like condiments than sauces. Creamy in texture, they are full of strong flavors and can be served as a garnish; or put a dollop on top of a plain grain dish to bring it into focus.

PROCEDURE
- Blend the oil and herbs together first, in a bowl with a fork or whisk or in a blender.
- Blend in liquids, then decorative vegetables.
- Store any leftover sauce in the refrigerator, tightly covered.

Cold Avocado Sauce

This sauce surprised me. I was playing with the idea that oil for a sauce could come from an oil-loaded vegetable like avocado. Fashioned after guacamole, this sauce is potent and zingy.

Yield: ¾ cup

2 cloves minced garlic
½ cup soft (ripe) avocado
2 tablespoons raspberry vinegar
1 teaspoon sea or vegetable salt
1 teaspoon prepared Dijon mustard
¼ cup white wine

1. Blend garlic and avocado. Add vinegar, salt, mustard, and wine.

SERVING SUGGESTIONS: I like this cold sauce on fresh, hot basmati rice, steeped with spices and decorated with peas and carrots.

Process

STYLE OF SAUCE: Vegetable topping.
BINDING AGENT: Avocado.
OIL: Avocado serves as both binding agent and oil. When using vegetables that don't have natural oil in them, add hazelnut, olive, or sesame oil.
COOKING LIQUID: Raspberry vinegar and white wine are accent liquids that also create substance. Lemon or tropical fruit juice could replace the wine.
HERBS AND SPICES: Garlic and prepared mustard flavor the sauce. Cilantro and tarragon would also be good flavors.

Tofu Mayonnaise

½ cup tofu
2 tablespoons apple cider
    vinegar
1 teaspoon sea salt
⅓ cup peanut oil
¼ teaspoon white pepper

Two key points hold true for making mayonnaise: One, don't try to make it in humid weather; the sun must be out or the proteins and oils don't bind. Two, pour the oil in very, very slowly. You will know if the sauce will thicken as soon as the oil goes in. Stop before all the oil goes in if you see the sauce is not binding.

Yield: ¾ cup

1. Boil tofu for 15 minutes. Press the excess liquid out and blend in a food processor or blender until it is very smooth.

2. Mix vinegar and salt into the tofu.

3. Very slowly, while blender is on, drip oil into the tofu until a thick mayonnaise substance appears.

4. Mix in pepper and store covered in the refrigerator.

Process

STYLE OF SAUCE: Vegetable topping.
BINDING AGENT: Tofu replaces eggs in this version of mayonnaise.
COOKING LIQUID: Apple cider vinegar is a neutral vinegar. For variety and interest, select raspberry or rice vinegar.
OIL: I used unrefined peanut oil and liked the quality of the final product. Safflower, light sesame, or olive oil each would work in the sauce; each will give it a slightly different flavor.
SALT SEASONING: Sea salt performs the function of salt without interfering with the taste. Light miso and umeboshi vinegar could be substitutes.
HERBS AND SPICES: Pepper was chosen for this variation. Basil, tarragon, thyme, garlic, curry, horseradish, and tomatoes are all possibilities.

Cold Olive Sauce

A black olive sauce will turn your grain dish purple. So instead of mixing it into the grain as a marinade, use it more as a relish or topping; mix it in while eating.

Yield: ½ cup

Blend garlic with olives and olive oil. Mix in vinegar, lemon juice, red pepper, and parsley.

SERVING SUGGESTIONS: This sauce works well with cooked teff. It can be mixed in; the color won't be a problem.

1 tablespoon minced garlic
3 tablespoons minced black Greek-style olives
1 tablespoon olive oil
2 tablespoons balsamic vinegar
4 tablespoons lemon juice
½ cup finely diced sweet red pepper
¼ cup minced parsley

Process

STYLE OF SAUCE: Vegetable topping.
BINDING AGENT: Olives; the meat of the olives makes a paste that serves as a base. Cooked puréed vegetables can also be a binding base.
COOKING LIQUID: The combination of balsamic vinegar and lemon juice makes a strong-flavored sauce. Any other vinegar would work, but pay attention to the vegetable base when making your selection.
OIL: Olive oil helps balance the strong cooking liquid and is most compatible with olive paste, the binding agent. Hazelnut oil and dark sesame make good alternatives, depending on the vegetable base.
SALT SEASONING: Olives, the star of this sauce, also play the role of salt seasoning. Look for nice plump brine-cured olives.
HERBS AND SPICES: For variations on this recipe, try basil, tarragon, or arugula.
VEGETABLES: Decorative vegetables, sweet red pepper and parsley, can be added to or replaced by slivers of carrot, green onions, or radishes.

Cold Mustard Sauce

1/3 cup raw cashews
1 cup water
2 teaspoons prepared
  mustard
1 tablespoon umeboshi
  paste

This sauce was invented for Baked Kasha With Turnips, but it would also be good on cooked vegetables and other first-stage cooked grains. In order to keep this a thin sauce I don't heat it. Heating will intensify the flavors and make it thick. (See hot nut sauces on pp. 155–58.)

Yield: 1 cup sauce (4–6 servings)

1. Whiz nuts and water together, making nut milk. Add the other ingredients and blend.

Process

STYLE OF SAUCE: Cold sauce.

BINDING AGENT: Options for this sauce are as varied as the choice of nuts in your pantry. See the Ingredients section (pp. 55, 57) for the qualities of each variety of nuts. Cashews become the binding agent in this recipe.

COOKING LIQUID: When water is combined with nuts, nut milk becomes the cooking liquid.

OIL: Nuts are oil.

SALT SEASONING: Umeboshi paste, that delightful seasoning that addresses both salty and sour tastes, makes this quick sauce delicious. If you don't have umeboshi paste, you might try umeboshi vinegar; or find a combination of salty and sour ingredients at hand, for example miso with vinegar or tamari with lemon juice.

OTHER FLAVORS: Prepared mustard accents and cuts through the heaviness of cashew oil. When making this style of cold sauce, you also might want to add sweeteners like rice syrup or honey, with or without the mustard.

Sesame Salt

Sesame seeds are rich in calcium. Their powerful food value is available to us only when the seeds are crushed because generally they are too small for us to chew. A small investment in a grinding tool may be worthwhile if you love this condiment or are interested in eating calcium-rich foods.

The best grinding tools are primitive mortar and pestle style bowls like a Japanese suribachi or a Mexican metate. These stone tools crush the oil of the seeds and the salt together. The blade of electric appliances can only cut the seeds, which doesn't release the oil or blend it well with the salt.

The amount of salt you choose depends on your diet and how you use this condiment. A salty ratio of 1 part salt to 10 parts seeds can be used as a salt seasoning in second-stage methods. A ratio of 1 part salt to 50 parts seeds makes a good table condiment. This recipe falls between those extremes.

2 teaspoons whole brown sesame seeds
1 teaspoon sea salt

1. Wash seeds as you would grain (see washing method on pp. 64–65). Drain.

2. Heat a heavy skillet over medium heat and add salt. Heat for 3 minutes, stirring to avoid browning. Grind salt to a fine powder in grinding bowl.

3. Heat skillet over medium-high heat and dry-roast seeds. When water has evaporated, lower heat to medium; adjust it to low as the seeds brown a bit and start to pop. They are done when you can crush them easily between thumb and forefinger and you can't help but notice the aroma.

4. Add the hot seeds to the crushed salt and press them against the sides of the bowl with the pestle until about 80 percent of the seeds have been crushed and the salt is distributed evenly throughout.

5. Store in an airtight glass or ceramic jar in a cool place.

Appendix

Cookware

I have a passion for cookware. I like it strong enough to endure my cooking adventures and attractive enough to show off the beauty of simple grains.

The following ideas will guide you in making decisions about purchasing and selecting cookware for whole-grain cookery. These choices are based on my experience and are not absolute. I have witnessed delicious dishes created from primitive kitchens and I wouldn't doubt there are useful modern inventions in progress as this book is being written.

Because the raw materials of this natural style of cooking are sensitive to their environment, the kind of cookware you choose is worthy of consideration. One of my long-time students has proven this very point with her experience. For five years Shelly had been cooking with information from classes; yet each time I saw her, she complained that nothing seemed to taste right or good. With each complaint I noticed that she included a hint about her cookware: the pot was bent, maybe the cover leaked steam, or the pot may have been too big for the burner. She also alluded to the fact that she hated her cookware. That impressed me most of all. When she found a gorgeous line of cookware that worked for her and the food, each dish became a revelation.

PURCHASING A STOVE

When choosing cookware, it is helpful to know the kind of heat source you will be cooking with. Is it gas, electric, open fire, or microwave? Before I get any further, I want to present my perspective on microwave cooking. I recognize this is an extremely time-efficient method. But since the heat (fire) source is so far removed from my senses (feeling of touch, smell, sight), I find it difficult to relate to as a natural cook. So I don't refer to microwave cooking at all. Open fire cooking is also not discussed in this book as it is no longer a common source of fire for everyday cooking. Gas heat allows us to see and feel exactly what we have; it is preferred for natural cooking because all our instincts can relate to it.

Geographically, gas may not be readily available, so some natural cooking enthusiasts hook up propane burners in order to feel a real flame. Electric stoves are second choice by default. Although we can feel their heat, a trusting relationship must be established between the cook and the dials.

If you have looked at new stoves, you will notice how the burners are placed close together with only one large burner and three small ones. Even though I know most household units are composed of one to four people (not large families), I can't help but feel this design is for heating packaged, frozen, and canned food. It is almost impossible to cook a full meal on small burners. The kind of cooking that is suggested in this book will have you cooking at least 1½ to 2 cups of grain and, more often than not, 3 cups of grain if you are the kind of cook who never has time to cook. If the burner is smaller than the pan, food won't cook evenly, so pots should fit the size of the burners.

CHOOSING COOKWARE

Grain cookery requires only a few pieces of cookware that are usually basic in any kitchen:

For cooking 1 to 3 cups of grain:

skillet (8″ or 10″)
casserole or dutch oven-style pot (3–6 quarts)
saucepan (1–3 quarts)
pressure cooker (6 quarts) is optional
glass bowls
baking dishes
wood or bamboo utensils

The size you choose will not only affect the amount of grain you can prepare, it may determine the kind of cooking methods that are possible. Valerie, an energetic new student and an excellent cook, told me of her first attempt at the boiling method. She left class eager to practice this unusual cooking method. Trying to ignore the workmen in the kitchen of her new apartment, she put the cooking liquid up to boil in a small pan. Her parents were expected shortly and she wanted to impress them with a new grain dish. The water boiled, the grain went in the water, and just as her parents came in, grain bubbled all over the new stove. This is one way to learn that the boiling method for grain needs a good-sized pot, at least large enough to hold eight parts of food and liquid, with room for bubbles.

The following list will give you an idea of the variety of cookware for each grain cooking method:

DRY-ROASTING—skillet, baking dish, pie plate, cookie sheet
SAUTÉING—skillet, saucepan, pressure cooker
SOAKING—saucepan, pressure cooker, glass bowl
BOILING—open saucepan (large)
BAKING—covered casserole or dutch oven
STEEPING—covered saucepan, casserole, or dutch oven, if
  they can be used stove-top
PRESSURE-COOKING—pressure cooker
MARINATING—glass bowl
DEEP-FRYING—skillet, dutch oven, stove-top casserole, wok
REFRYING—skillet
BRAISING—skillet with cover

I try to purchase cookware that is gorgeous and functional. I want to be able to sauté in it, cook in it stove-top and/or in the oven, and still have it be beautiful enough to serve in. The materials to choose from can be confusing. For natural food cooking, heavy-gauge cookware is preferable. A heavy bottom allows sautéing and reduces the risk of burning but most importantly creates even, steady cooking. A cover that is heavy enough to create a seal prevents moisture and heat loss. The basic design of handles and balance of weight should fit you, your hand, and your strength. Perhaps the most important criterion for good cookware is how it responds to fire (the heat source). No matter which kind of cookware you choose, your understanding of how it holds and responds to heat and moisture is paramount.

CAST-IRON COOKWARE has been my all-time favorite. One of my pots is over 100 years old. Shaped as a dutch oven, this black beauty is used for dry-roasting, sautéing, steeping, baking, deep-frying, refrying, and braising. It is the ultimate in weighty cookware; no steam escapes the heavy lid, and the forearms of the cook become very strong. My 10-inch skillet is only twenty years old, but it handles most of the cooking, dry-roasting, refrying, deep-frying and braising grain as well as different sauces. Originally cast-iron cookware was made for wood stoves. With about 3 percent carbon alloy, cast-iron cookware can handle very high temperatures and emits a slight amount of iron into the food, providing a shade of dietary iron. Occasionally this rusty-looking element lines the pan. Curing these pots with oil creates a good seal and prolongs the life of the cookware as well as reducing the risk of foods sticking. Oil the pan after each use, especially following a cooking method that doesn't use oil.

Enamel-coated cast-iron pans are lined with porcelain clay. It creates a smooth surface that doesn't need curing and gives the black pot an opportunity for modern glamour and design. Natural food loves to be next to the porcelain clay from earth. Porcelain-lined cast iron has been my preferred cookware for years and I love my new pressure cooker that is steel with several coats of blue porcelain. The only disadvantage to porcelain cookware is that it chips easily, especially when zealous cooks hit metal spoons against the edge of the pot or the pot becomes a receptacle for soaking dishes and knives. Minor chips and nicks are not serious, but should there be many or large areas where the porcelain has been scratched away, the pot could cause problems. With care these pots can last at least fifteen years.

STAINLESS STEEL COOKWARE. This was developed to eliminate the problems of cast iron. They are known for their shiny smooth and constant surface and lighter weight. Today there is a great variety. Some are built to last a lifetime and others will endure perhaps seven years. My observation of this kind of cookware is that the long-lasting designs are heavy gauged, priced at the high end, and usually beautifully designed with considerations for serving, dripless pouring, stacking, and storing. They have welded-on handles. The short-life versions fade in beauty, even the pretty copper bottoms, have thin walls and loose covers. If you choose stainless steel cookware for natural food cooking, look for pots with copper or aluminum inlaid bottoms. These will insure even cooking.

GLASS COOKWARE. The major drawback is that it breaks. It breaks if there is a weakness in the glass, if the temperature changes too rapidly, and, of course, in any major collision or impact. Adding liquid to a hot, dry pan will crack the glass and a simple chip on the rim will prevent a good seal. These pans retain heat for a long time. Especially good on glass-topped stoves, this cookware is responsive to natural food. I like to watch the food cook in them; there is no need to remove the cover to see what is happening. I recommend that you don't deep-fry in glass cookware.

ALUMINUM COOKWARE is inexpensive and thin. These pots dent easily, causing uneven cooking. Should the stove heat unevenly, this cookware will develop hot spots and areas may burn. The surface is not totally resistant to exchanging elements with certain foods. Although this element is useful for humans, too much aluminum can be dangerous. Avoid aluminum cookware.

Teflon-coated or metal cookware that boast nonstick surfaces repel me, as my experience in cooking with them showed me that natural foods don't relate to this kind of cookware at all. They must be designed for meat and cheese cookery (we all know how hard it is to remove baked or burnt cheese and animal fat from cookware). These pots scratch easily, and food sticks to the scratches.

PRESSURE COOKERS. I find a pressure cooker is indispensable for grain cookery not so much to shorten the cooking time as to create a texture that is impossible to achieve by any other cooking method. There is a great selection of pressure cookers; stainless steel or steel with porcelain linings are superior if they are heavy gauged at least at the bottom. Some stainless-steel pressure cookers have a thin bottom and are indented for some reason. Grain cooks unevenly and usually burns in this kind of cooker. All modern pressure cookers have safety valves to prevent blow-ups. Most won't even open until the pressure inside has returned to normal. If you like grain croquettes (deep-fried), then you will want a pressure cooker. Because grain cooks in steam in this method, you can use much less water than other methods.

UTENSILS, BOWLS, AND GADGETS. Bamboo and wood utensils are great for stirring, dry-roasting, and serving. They carry the vibration of the cooking food to the cook. This helps determine when the food is done. Nonmetal utensils are more gentle with the food and less likely to break, cut, or tear through cooked food. The exceptions to this preference are good, flexible stainless steel spatula and whisk.

Glass, stainless steel, and wood bowls and containers suit grains more than plastic utensils and storage containers. Their natural affinity will become clear as you work with grains.

The most important gadget in the grain cookery kitchen is a flame tamer, sometimes known as a flame deflector or heat diffuser. True to its name, this instrument disperses direct heat and prevents burning. I suggest you use it when steeping or pressure-cooking and for maintaining sauce temperatures.

STRAINERS. The smaller the holes in the strainer the easier it will be to strain small grains and seeds. Choose a 6- to 8-inch strainer for draining washed grains. A small 3- to 4-inch flat oil skimmer is useful in deep-frying.

GINGER GRATER. This specialty tool breaks up the fiber of fresh ginger root. Choose a ginger grater that has a trough to catch the juice and is tall enough for lengthy strides. Squeeze the fiber together to release the juice.

VEGETABLE KNIFE. A good vegetable knife has a very thin, sharp edge. Japanese vegetable knives are my favorite shape—long blades made for slicing, not chopping. These blades measure 6½ inches by almost 2 inches and that's just the blade; the handle holds the blade with steel rivets. I find both carbon and molybdenum steel hold a good edge and sharpen easily on porcelain, either on the bottom of a coffee mug or a porcelain sharpening rod. The secret to keeping the edge sharp is to wash, dry, and put it away immediately after each use.

BLENDERS AND FOOD PROCESSORS. These are optional. They are great for quantity cooking and save a lot of time and effort in sauce cookery.

I have listed the few kitchen items whose function can't be replaced with eating utensils, like forks, butter knives, teaspoons, and coffee or tea mugs. For example, I use a coffee mug to measure grain and cooking liquid, a fork for teasing the juice out of a lemon, and teaspoons and soup spoons for estimated measuring when I think I need to have some idea of ratios.

Since my kitchen is too small for the amount of cookware I enjoy collecting, I want to stress that grain cookery really needs only a few special pieces. Simplifying equipment will be helpful when organizing the kitchen flow.

CHART OF EQUIVALENTS

Use this guide to practice cooking with whole decorative vegetables. It will help you learn to judge quantities without measuring.

	½ tsp.	1 tsp.	1 T.	¼ cup	½ cup	1 cup
ONION						
juice		⅛ sm.	¼ sm.			
diced				½ sm.	1 sm.	1 lg.
CARROT						
diced				1 sm.	1 med.	1 lg.
CELERY						
diced				1 rib	2 ribs	4 ribs
GREEN ONION						
sliced small				1 med.	2 med.	4 med.
SWEET PEPPER						
diced				⅛ med.	¼ med.	½ med.
GARLIC CLOVES						
minced	1 sm.	1 med.	1 lg.			
GINGER						
juice			1″ × 1″			
minced			1″ × 1″			

FIRST-STAGE COOKING METHODS WORKSHEET

NAME OF GRAIN _____   amount _____

TEXTURE _____

PRELIMINARY TREATMENT _____

1ST-STAGE COOKING METHOD _____

    Cooking liquid _____   amount _____

    Temperature liquid/grain _____

SEASONINGS

    Oil _____   amount _____

    Salt _____   amount _____

    Herbs/Spices _____

    _____

VEGETABLES _____   amount _____

    _____

    _____

DECORATIVE _____

    _____

    _____

NOTES:

NAME OF DISH _____

SECOND-STAGE COOKING METHODS WORKSHEET

NAME OF GRAIN _____

1ST-STAGE COOKING METHOD _____   cooking liquid _____

     Preliminary treatments _____   _____

2ND-STAGE COOKING METHOD _____

     Cooking liquid _____   amount _____

     Oil _____   amount _____

     Salt _____   amount _____

     Herbs/spices _____
     _____
     _____

     Miscellaneous _____
     _____

VEGETABLES _____
_____
_____

DECORATIVE _____
_____
_____

_____

NOTES:

NAME OF DISH _____

HOT SAUCE WORKSHEET

STYLE OF SAUCE _____

BINDING AGENT _____

COOKING LIQUID _____

OIL _____

SALT SEASONING _____

HERBS/SPICES _____

_____

NOTES:

SERVED WITH _____

COLD SAUCE WORKSHEET

STYLE OF SAUCE _____

COOKING LIQUID _____

OIL _____

SALT SEASONING _____

HERBS/SPICES _____

BINDING AGENT (for mayonnaise-style sauces) _____

_____

NOTES:

SERVED WITH _____

Anatomy of a Grain

Whole grains are made up of three parts: the pericarp, the endosperm, and the germ.

There are seven layers in a whole grain, each having an important function. The pericarp, the outermost layer, is made up of three parts: the epicarp, a sometimes waxy coating that contacts the hull if there is one; the mesocarp, a fleshy layer; and the endocarp, made up of tubelike cells that contain pigment.

The next four layers make up the endosperm. Aleurone, containing protein, oil, minerals, and enzymes, is followed by three layers of starch granules embedded in a protein matrix: peripheral, corneous, and floury in the center.

The germ is composed of two major parts: the embryonic axis, which is concerned with root development and growth, and the scutellum, which stores oil, protein, enzymes, and minerals.

Resource: Dr. Lloyd Rooney and Dr. Sergio O. Serna-Saldivar, "Cereal Quality Laboratory Report," Department of Soil and Crop Sciences, Texas A&M University.

ANATOMY OF A GRAIN

The dish grains in this book are of the caryopsis style of seed. This is a structure where the pericarp is bonded to the endosperm as opposed to the utricle style of seed where the pericarp attaches only at one point on the endosperm (foxtail, finger millet).

1. Pericarp
   epicarp—waxy outermost edge
   mesocarp—fleshy layer
   endocarp—hard leathery tube cells where pigment is
      located
2. Endosperm
   Aleurone—protein, oil, minerals, and enzymes
   Peripheral—starch granules embedded in a protein
      matrix
   Corneous—starch granules embedded in protein matrix
   Floury—where gluten, starch live
3. Germ—Cells of energy of reproduction

GENERAL ANATOMY OF A GRAIN

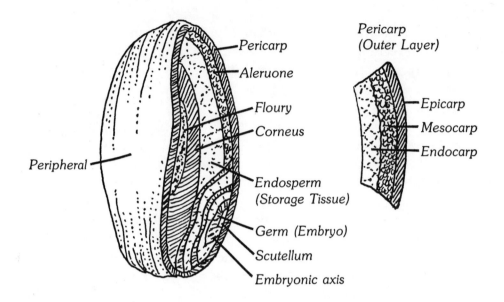

Peripheral

Pericarp

Aleruone

Floury

Corneus

Endosperm
(Storage Tissue)

Germ (Embryo)

Scutellum

Embryonic axis

Pericarp
(Outer Layer)

Epicarp

Mesocarp

Endocarp

ABOUT THE AUTHOR

Joanne Saltzman is founder and director of the School of Natural Cookery in Boulder, Colorado. With more than 20 years' experience cooking natural foods, she writes a cooking column, "The Natural Cook," for *Nexus,* a Colorado bimonthly, and gives lectures and cooking seminars. She lives in Boulder with her four children and is in the process of certification by the Transformational Healing Institute to further her work as a healer.

For information on the cooking school or how you can teach "the process" in your area, call the School of Natural Cookery at (303) 444-8068.

INDEX